BEYOND THE NOTES

This book is dedicated to my daughters Julia, Rachel and late daughter Kathryn, also my grandchildren Dan, Lucy, Henry, Harvey, Skye, Daisy and Charlie.

*   *   *

All profits from this book will be donated to the Gwyn Williams Bursary for young string players.

BEYOND THE NOTES

A LIFELONG PASSION
FOR CLASSICAL MUSIC

STEPHANNIE WILLIAMS

BREWIN BOOKS

BREWIN BOOKS
19 Enfield Ind. Estate,
Redditch,
Worcestershire,
B97 6BY
www.brewinbooks.com

Published by Brewin Books 2020

A CIP catalogue record for this book is
available from the British Library.

ISBN: 978-1-85858-716-5

Printed and bound in Great Britain by
Hobbs The Printers Ltd.

CONTENTS

ACKNOWLEDGMENTS

The author is eternally grateful to the following people; Christopher Morley, Nick Bailey, Andrew Baker, Margaret Baker, Sir Humphrey Burton, Tom Collard, Anne Hobbs, David Jones, Andrew Jowett OBE, Eric Labrum, John Lill CBE, Dame Felicity Lott, Sir Simon Rattle, Dennis and Diane Ricketts, John Ricketts, Edward Smith, Kevin Whately, Jane Woolfenden and Simon Wright.

FOREWORD

Steve (Stephannie) is one of the few really respectful and respected of Artist's Managers. Devoted, determined, dedicated, ambitious (for them, not herself!) and someone with whom I always enjoyed engaging in discussions during my 21 years with the CBSO. Not only were they productive, but also fun.

As an almost one-woman band she initiated and managed so many projects with her artists and ensembles with all the care and attention which many with far bigger resources could learn from as a model. And by not seeking to expand her business (which she probably could have done) she was able to focus on her select group and give them her personal advice, support and service from which they all benefitted. She was trusted by both them and 'us'!

As one of her first 'clients' as the violist in the Arioso Quartet, Gwyn, her husband, was a recipient of her early experience as an agent. His musicianship, collegial temperament and dedication to both the CBSO and the Quartet were so valuable to both ensembles and he and Steve's time together devoted to music making in Birmingham and the wider world are still very fondly remembered by so many.

Edward Smith
Chief Executive CBSO 1978-1999

"My Musical Family..."

*   *   *

Richard Baker, much-loved newsreader, broadcaster and presenter once commented to me, "Steve, you have met and worked with so many fascinating people, and tell such amazing anecdotes. Why don't you turn it all into a book?"

And here it is.

*   *   *

I am very grateful to Christopher Morley, Chief Music Critic of the *Birmingham Post*, and my friend and colleague for over thirty years, for agreeing to be my editor and collaborator. My thanks also for the many great reviews he has written of my amazing adventures over the years.

Chapter 1

FROM WINDSOR TO POZNAN

I put the telephone down from The Civil Aviation Authority and was both relieved and excited. I had managed to divert a Lot Airlines flight to stop at Poznan airport on its way from Warsaw to Heathrow. Quite some achievement in communist Poland in the 1980s!

How did all this come about and why was it necessary to do this?

Representing the Queen's Choir of St George's Chapel, Windsor was prestigious but also quite a responsibility.

I had been called by the Director of the Poznan Festival in Poland to ask if the boys of St George's Chapel could represent the UK in his festival of boys' choirs from around the world. Christopher Robinson, the then Director of music at Windsor Castle said this would be fine once okayed by the Windsor powers that be, but only if we could also take the lay clerks to sing in a concert with the boys. I agreed that this was necessary and eventually all was finalised. The boys could sing in a festival concert but the closing event of the Festival would be a performance of Handel's 'Messiah' with the choruses sung by the full St George's choir.

There were many arrangements to be made for this visit to Poland but as the time drew near it transpired that following 'Messiah' on the final night of the festival, the choir would need to travel through the night from Poznan to Warsaw to catch the early morning flight back to Heathrow. This seemed quite unreasonable for boys aged 7-12 but the Festival Director would not budge. What was I to do now?

I decided to try something utterly impossible. I called my friend, Captain Clarke from British Airways "How difficult would it be to divert a Lot airline plane?" I asked. He replied "with difficulty Stephannie". After hearing my story he thought for a moment and then said "the first thing to do is to get the flight path diverted and then get Lot Airlines to agree to divert the plane". He gave me the name of the person to contact at the Civil Aviation Authority to discuss diverting the flight path and wished me luck.

I started my task by calling the CAA and by this time my story was growing. I said that there would be great unrest at the Castle if these young boys had to travel through the night to get the flight home. After all, this choir was representing the UK in a communist country together with the Vienna Boys Choir, Copenhagen Boys Choir etc. This flight problem was happening a week before the Festival so time was not on our side.

My contact at CAA however, could not have been more helpful and told me to leave it with him and he would see what he could do, but there was only a very slim chance and he would call me back. The eagerly-awaited call came two days later and to my utter amazement he gave me the news that the flight path had been changed!

This of course was just the start, because with only a few days to spare I had to get Lot Airlines to agree to divert the flight. This meant getting on a train to London to see the MD of Lot Airlines. My anxiety was growing even more, but the MD was charming and said that he would see what he could do. He called Lot in Warsaw and then told me he had been very persuasive as far as his colleagues in Poland were concerned but I would not know the position for sure until Saturday, the day of our departure from the UK. When we arrived in Poznan on Saturday my first job, with heart in mouth, was to visit Lot Airlines in the main square. Once again my luck was in and I was told that due to exceptional circumstances the airline had agreed to divert the plane.

On the day of our return to the UK our party of sixteen boys, twelve lay clerks, the organist, Director of Music, headmaster and matron from the choir school, plus yours truly, arrived at Poznan airport at 7am. I was feeling very nervous – what if the plane did not arrive and we were all left stranded at Poznan airport! I was responsible for over thirty people getting back to Windsor Castle of all places! Suddenly one of the boys shouted "Mrs Williams, Mrs Williams the plane's coming" and sure enough there was a large plane coming down to land on a very small runway.

We all had to carry our cases out to the plane to be loaded into the hold and then we boarded. We then heard disgruntled business men strongly complaining "this flight should be direct to London why have we come down in Poznan?" Luckily as soon as we were in the air the pilot made an announcement to say that Lot Airlines were very honoured to have the Royal Choir of St George's Chapel, Windsor Castle travelling on this flight and we had dropped down in Poznan to pick them up.

A great cheer followed and then a round of applause. We decided this was good enough for the choir to sing for these diverted tolerant business men.

On arrival back in Windsor Christopher commented "I shall let them know about this up at the Castle".

The above was only one of the challenges and experiences with this eventful visit to communist Poland. We stayed in a decent hotel and were given zlotys subsistence daily. The boys had never seen such money because there were hundreds of zlotys to a pound at that time. They discovered that they could buy more sweets with the money than they could ever have imagined and they needed to spend the money because Polish currency could not be taken out of the country.

All went well with the boys' concert and then preparation started for the grand closing event of 'Messiah'. There was a morning rehearsal, and on the afternoon of the final day a grand reception was given for all the choirs, amounting to several hundred people. The reception was very lavish by communist standards and a number of speeches were made.

I was becoming slightly concerned because in my contract, there was an agreement that I would receive the choir fee in Sterling prior to the evening performance and so far nothing had been mentioned. I decided the time had come to approach the Festival Director, who was most dismissive and I was told he would deal with the matter later. The afternoon was then turning into early evening and I knew the choir would be departing shortly for the church. By this time I had approached the director several times and he was obviously getting very irritated with me.

The coach arrived to transport the choir – time for action! I instructed the choir not to sing until I arrived at the church with the fee, which was quite substantial. I then sought out the Director and told him that the choir had been instructed not to sing until I had arrived at the church with the money. A very irate director asked me to follow him to his office but he informed me he only had dollars. Getting out my calculator I worked out how many thousand dollars I would need in place of the Sterling. He opened the safe and took out wads of dollars, which we counted out until we reached the correct sum. I then stuffed all these dollars into my large briefcase, thanked him for the money and rushed out of the office.

The next problem was to work out how I would get to the church. I needn't have worried because a young Pole came up to me and said "Mrs Williams, your coach is waiting". I had visions of a horse-drawn carriage but was led to a 50-seater coach which was for me alone, and I was transported to the church in solitary splendour!

Crowds were pouring into the church by the time I arrived and I had to push my way through the masses, holding my briefcase, full of dollars, tightly to my chest. I eventually arrived at the vestry where all members of the choir were waiting eagerly to hear if they would be singing or not on that final festival concert. I held up the briefcase and said "I have the money!" Following a round of applause from the choir, one of the lay clerks informed me that television cameras were present and we had not discussed TV. This was in breach of our contract and had not been mentioned in any of the negotiations. At this stage there was nothing I could do so I turned to the choir and said "I am afraid you will have to go and sing and pretend you haven't seen the cameras".

The concert was a great success and I had not heard this brilliant choir sing better. The orchestra was very good and conducted superbly by Christopher. All the excellent soloists were foreign, which had presented a few problems in rehearsal but all this was overcome. However, Christopher had never experienced a male soprano before, as we had on this occasion, although he had worked with countertenors, and in particular Michael Chance, in the past. Christopher was rather thrown at the first rehearsal with the soloists but when he realised that it was such a good soprano there was no problem. The only rather disconcerting thing about the performance was the fact that the male soprano and countertenor congratulated each other adoringly after each other's solos!

All in all it was one of the most eventful tours of my amazing career.

Chapter 2

WAR YEARS – CHILDHOOD
AND TRINITY COLLEGE OF MUSIC

I was born just after the commencement of World War II so these were turbulent years especially living a few miles from Woolwich Arsenal, Vickers Armstrong and Burndebts ammunition factory, where my mother worked during the war. These three were all major targets for the Germans. My brother John and I were not evacuated as my parents decided if we were to be bombed we should all go together!

Most people had an underground air raid shelter but my father had built an Anderson brick shelter in the garden where we all departed as soon as we heard the sirens. All, that is, apart from brother John, four years older than me. As soon as he heard the siren he disappeared. He would run to meet with his friends and dash off to a large bombed house in Barnehurst, climb onto the roof and wait for the doodlebugs to drop.

There was a scary long drone from the doodlebug as it was approaching and then, as soon as the drone stopped there was a deathly silence as the flying bomb made its descent followed by a huge explosion. The boys would watch to see where the bomb had dropped and then rushed to the crater, if it was close by, as it inevitably was. They would climb into the crater and toss the hot shrapnel to each other until the Home Guard arrived. The Dad's Army soldiers would look down into the crater and say "It's those buggers again" and then chase them off.

I have memories of VE Day in 1945 when there were street parties everywhere celebrating the end of WWII. There was a fancy dress competition after afternoon tea and my mother, always wanting to make an impression, dressed me as a sugar cube because of my very blonde hair. I wore a cardboard top hat with cotton wool balls stuck over it. My dress of white crepe paper, not too difficult to come by in the war, and white shoes covered in cotton wool balls completed the outfit. I suppose the cotton wool balls represented the sugar cubes! It must have been a good outfit because I won first prize and was made to stand on a trestle table for a photograph.

Later that evening I watched the dancing in the street from my open bedroom window. Due to bombings all the glass had been blown out of the windows. I vaguely remember a night of unexpected bombings when the glass from a window shattered all over me in bed and my father had to pick out the glass from around me, after he had told me to stay very still so as not to be cut by the glass.

My father was a carpenter, master craftsman and cabinetmaker so in the war he was enlisted to work on the Mosquitos because the frame was constructed mainly of wood. The Mosquito was named The Wooden Wonder or 'Mossie' to its crew. Working on these fighter planes was crucial wartime work. When I look back I think how clever my father was because he could carve and make things from any piece of wood. All our Christmas presents were home-made. My brother had a fantastic rocking horse carved from one piece of wood and another year I had a magnificent double fronted Doll's House.

My father built a yacht when he was a young man and sailed to France with his friends. My grandmother on Dad's side was French so my father was very much drawn to visiting France. My great-grandmother came to England with Madame Tussaud, as her maid. They arrived in London on Lord Mayor's Day when everyone was celebrating and my great-grandmother thought the English were all mad! Madame Tussaud gave my great-grandmother a gift of a silver fob watch when she left her service and went on to work for Lady Cobham. I still have that watch in my possession to this day.

My father also regaled us with stories of the events he attended and people he saw when he was young, these included Houdini, Paul Robeson and Buffalo Bill. He told of Houdini being chained, put into a crate and lowered down into the Thames. My father was watching on the riverside and saw him surface within a few minutes, swim to the bank and climb up, close by my father, to great cheers from the crowds. He also told us of hearing the great voice of Paul Robeson singing 'Ol' Man River' in the Woolwich Hippodrome. Paul Robeson was one of my Dad's great heroes. Another memory of his was going to the Erith recreation ground to see Buffalo Bill's Wild West Show.

It was still wartime when I started ballet lessons. My mother had been a local dance teacher and wanted to be a ballerina but due to circumstances never had the opportunity to pursue a career. I think due to this she was very ambitious for me and decided I should have ballet lessons with Katie Huxtable. I was never very interested in ballet and spent most of the lessons looking at myself in the wall to wall mirrors, which apparently I found fascinating! I was however included in a ballet performance at Northumberland Heath Secondary School Hall, which was one of the best halls in the area still standing. I was, at three years old, one of the fairies and had to dance round in a circle three times. I found this rather good and decided three times was not enough so, when the other fairies had stopped dancing, I decided to continue going round in spite of the hisses "Stephannie stop now". The more the audience laughed the more I enjoyed it and decided to keep going! I was only stopped by the warning siren. We were hastily ushered off the stage and down into the underground shelter so there was no end to my debut performance.

It was after this incident my mother decided I should end my short ballet career. She told Miss Huxtable that I was much too heavy on my feet and also too plump so she was not going to waste her money on ballet lessons for Stephannie.

It was not until I was eight years old that piano lessons started and this was just after my younger brother Dennis was born. We had a very nice upright piano inherited from my grandmother but I was never allowed to play on this instrument so I pretended the table was a piano and played up and down on the table! Eventually my mother decided I should have piano lessons but, although we were not well off, I would go to the best teacher in the area Mr Thomas Eastop. I really enjoyed piano lessons and made good progress, much to the delight of my mother, who then decided, if I could not be ballerina I would be a concert pianist! Thomas Eastop held a music appreciation class every Tuesday night at Shornells, Abbey Wood. I was taken to this class every Tuesday by my mother, even though I was the only child attending. This proved to be good for me because, as I progressed with my piano lessons, I was encouraged to perform occasionally at the class to the adult audience. Shornells had a yearly trip to the opera at Sadlers Wells and of course I was included in the trip and my first opera 'Don Giovanni' made a great impression on me.

A big upset came when Thomas Eastop died suddenly of a heart attack when I was fourteen. An ex pupil of Thomas took over the Shornells music appreciation class and I was then sent to him for piano lessons. Disaster! I began to hate music lessons because I was wrapped over the knuckles frequently and could never do anything to please. For two years no progress was made and my mother was furious with me because I did not want to practise. I eventually convinced her that I should leave this teacher and find someone else. We found lovely Winifred Scott, a brilliant piano teacher who lived in Bexleyheath, only a fifteen minute bus ride from my home in Barnehurst. Winifred decided I should take Grade V theory and Grade VIII piano as soon as my lessons started with her. When I was nine I had won first prize in a talent competition playing Beethoven's 'Fur Elise' at Saturday morning pictures and also a bronze medal from an LCM exam but I had never taken any Associated Board examinations and theory was something quite new to me.

At around this time I was being asked to perform in concerts at my very good school Bexley Technical College for girls where I was working for GCE exams. Another pupil at the school, Kathleen Gilbert, was around the same piano standard and we often played together. Kathleen did not go into the music profession but we remain good friends to this day. We were both asked to perform at Dartford Grammar School where Denis Matthews was coming to judge a piano competition with pianists from the area. I was awarded a prize by Denis Matthews at this competition and also given the chance to attend a Music course in Matlock, Derbyshire funded by Maidstone County Council. I think this Music course was a turning point in my musical career and made me determined to follow the music route in some way. Most of the students on the course were from the North of England but mainly from Liverpool. I was ribbed mercilessly about my Southern accent and the way I said 'bath' and 'laugh' among other words.

I did not know at the time that I was being tutored by some of the greatest musicians of the time, Harold Craxton, Dame Myra Hess, Harry Isaacs, Colin Horsley and Denis Matthews to name but a few. A piano recital given one evening by Dame Myra Hess made a lasting impression on me and I decided that I definitely wanted to pursue a musical career. It was not all work but some play and I had many enjoyable walks over the heather with the other students singing part songs and rounds as we walked, receiving strange glances from everyone we passed. One night six of us decided to slip out of our rooms and climb up the hill to the ruined Riber Castle, known by the locals as Smedley's Folly and thought to be haunted. We arrived at the castle at around midnight but found it so spooky that the six of us took flight and ran down the hill back to our digs as fast as we could. It took us some time to work out how to climb back into our locked digs without being discovered. We did eventually manage to find an open window and climb back in but it was all quite an adventure, which always remained a secret to my parents. What a week that was!

It was about this time that I joined the church choir in Abbey Wood with choir master John Palmer, father of the internationally-renowned singer Dame Felicity Palmer. I also started organ lessons with Mr Palmer, who was a lovely man, fine musician and great teacher. I was sixteen at this time and Felicity was about twelve. We both sang alto in the choir and I kept an eye on Felicity to make sure she was okay because she was the youngest alto, the others apart from me, were boys around my age or older. The sopranos were young choir boys and the tenors and basses consisted of elderly gentlemen from the area. Abbey Wood was quite a long way from Barnehurst, where we lived at the time, and I had to make a bus ride of at least 45 minutes to get to Abbey Wood.

My father disapproved of make-up but I wanted to wear make-up to look good for choir practices, because of the boys! On the bus to Abbey Wood I grabbed an upstairs seat at the back and applied my secretly bought make-up. What my parents did not know was that on a Friday Choir practice night at the C of E Church of St Michael's, it was also Youth Club Night at the Methodist Church Hall, a short distance from St Michael's. As soon as practice was over I went with the boys, not Felicity, to the Methodist Youth Club where we enjoyed a Rock and Roll evening to Lonnie Donegan, Elvis Presley and other pop music. Rock and Roll was all the rage at this time and it was great fun being swung into the air with petticoats flying. At about 10pm I thought it time to leave and get my bus back to Barnehurst carefully removing my make-up in the back upstairs seat. On return home my father would query the long choir practice but I told him he should understand that we did have a lot of music to rehearse. I don't think my parents ever knew I had such a great time at the Methodist Youth Club on Friday evenings after choir practice!

It was at this time in 1955 when my brother John enlisted into the Royal West Kent's to do his National Service. He was a great fitness fanatic and wanted to become a PTI but was told that he would have to sign up for three years so this is what he did. He was sent to Shornecliffe near Folkestone for four weeks training and then the regiment moved to Dover Castle. The regiment was later moved to Salisbury Plain but John stayed in Dover to finish his PTI course. On successfully finishing the course he went to Aldershot to the Second Paratroopers regiment for Para training. It was at this stage his clothes were sent back in a parcel and we were informed that he was now serving abroad. He had in fact been sent out on HMS Devonshire to Port Said and we later discovered that he had been fighting in the Suez Crisis with the Nasser problem. The fighting only lasted seven days and from Egypt he was then sent to Cyprus to join the Royal West Kents in Famagusta for the EOKA problem with Archbishop Makarios and General Grivas, which lasted for many months. Next followed the Troodos Mountains to fight a huge forest fire. It was a tough three years for John but he returned home as a Sergeant. I think he would have stayed in the army if it had not been for romance and I was responsible for that!

Irene Smith, one of my friends at school, asked if she could write to my brother. As he was fighting abroad she felt sure a few letters from England would cheer him up and, although we had no idea where he was, we could send letters and parcels to be forwarded through BFPO. The correspondence between the two grew into a huge romance and on his return home John asked Irene to marry him. This presented problems at home because my mother disapproved for no good reason and Irene's Mum was a Catholic. It was very rare in those days for a Protestant to marry a Catholic but John was determined and the two married in 1960 without my parents' presence and much against Irene's mother's will. At this time John was an apprentice compositor. He worked his way through all aspects of printing and, after a few years, started his own successful printing business with Irene as the administrator and financial wizard. They had four lovely children but sadly Irene passed away with cancer at the early age of fifty four. John and I, although never very close in childhood, are now very close. John, now retired, lives in Maidstone and has nine grandchildren and three great grandchildren to keep him busy.

We have now come to my entry into Trinity College of Music. My father had told me that when I reached eighteen I was on my own and I had to support myself. Although having achieved the necessary education qualifications I would have to apply for a grant to enter music college if this is what I wanted. I applied for a major award from Maidstone County Council and I was given a rigorous interview besides being asked to perform on the piano and organ. Fortunately I obtained a major award which paid for my fees and travel so, if I got a job at weekends, I would be able to enter Trinity College of Music. I did a variety of jobs during my three years at Trinity, which included car valeting, shop assistant in Woolworths and engraving names on Parker pens in a stationers shop to pay for my keep at home.

I entered Trinity in September 1958 and was very fortunate to have Janet Barker as my piano tutor, James Gaddarn for singing and John Webster on organ. I now felt I had made a good start towards a music profession and I was aiming for LTCL and GTCL teachers diplomas. There were brilliant class tutors at that time including Gladys Puttick, Cyril Cork, Lettice Ward and Charles Proctor to name but a few. Dr Greenhouse Allt was Principal of the college during this period.

My first year was the time I found that I was a good organiser of events! At the end of every year Trinity College held a ball at Caxton Hall for students and the first year students were expected to provide the cabaret on that evening. I was given the job of organising this cabaret in June 1959. My first job was to find suitable first year students who would be willing to participate. One of the items I decided, besides other offerings, there would be a performance of Offenbach's Can Can with frou frou skirts and splits at the end! To find likely candidates, not necessarily for the Can Can, I thought I would go down to the basement of Trinity where it housed the library and an excellent games room complete with table tennis facilities. Two lads were playing table tennis and one of the lads, tall, dark and good looking appeared to be a likely candidate so between a lull in the game I went up to him to ask if he was a first year. He looked scornfully down at me and informed me that he was a fifth year! I apologised profusely and departed in haste thinking what an arrogant person he was but little was I to know that this would be my husband for over fifty-three wonderful years.

Footnote – My name
Why was I called Stephannie with two 'n's? I inherited the name from my mother but, when she was born, her parents had a great friend called Steve and another called Annie so these two names were put together – hence Stephannie!

Chapter 3

MOVING FORWARD

At the end of my first year at Trinity College I encountered the arrogant young man again! I was in the rather crowded common room waiting for a lecture when a soldier in full army uniform came into the room. There were shouts of "It's Gwyn". He was obviously very popular but I recognised him as the table tennis player I had seen a few weeks earlier and thought "oh no, not him!"

It appeared he had just finished his National Service training and had come into college to see his friends. In addition he had been offered a scholarship from Trinity College for violin lessons as long as he led the college orchestra. After training in Oswestry he was sent to Woolwich Barracks where he played in the very prestigious Woolwich Artillery Band under Major Hayes. He played violin in the orchestra and Alto saxophone in the band.

Gwyn had violin lessons at Trinity initially with Yfrah Neaman and then with Jan Sedivka. He also won the Alfred Gibson Award in his last year, which was awarded to the best student of the year.

Gwyn played alto sax in the Woolwich Artillery band and also in the marching band. He played for many important occasions such as the Cup Final and at Buckingham Palace when the Queen was presented with a brooch after the birth of Prince Andrew. It was at this prestigious event that he was confined to barracks for a week because he sneezed on parade due to his hay fever!

Back to my subsequent meetings with Gwyn following his appearance on that day. Gwyn was given time off from the band to attend his violin lessons at Trinity and to play in the college orchestra, which meant he frequently turned up at college. Everywhere I went he seemed to pop up and one day he asked me if I would go to Richmond with him on the following Sunday. I already had an on and off boyfriend at college who was a pianist and composer so I declined at first but

Gwyn was very persistent so eventually I agreed. He said he would meet me at 11am under the clock at Charing Cross Station.

I arrived at the station just before 11am and waited and waited. I was beginning to feel rather cross and thinking I would not wait any longer when he came running up to me full of profuse apologies. It appeared someone had thrown themselves onto the tube line so the tube had to wait in the tunnel for nearly an hour while they cleared the line. After this incident Gwyn was very nervous of confined spaces and would rarely travel in the tube or take a lift.

We took a train to Richmond and, as it was a beautiful day, spent the rest of the day in the park and by the river. I understood at this time why Gwyn was so popular with everyone because he was such a kind, sensitive and considerate person with a great personality. By the end of the day we were madly in love with each other and I had the onerous task of telling my boyfriend the next day that it was all off as far as we were concerned. Fortunately I don't think he was too bothered because it was more off than on! I was however the envy of many of the girls at Trinity College because Gwyn was so popular, talented and handsome.

After our Richmond day Gwyn frequently came to college to meet me and travel back to my home in Bexleyheath. We would spend the evening playing violin and piano duos. Whenever the music stopped my young brother, who was then ten years old, was sent to ask if we would like a cup of tea. On one or two occasions he asked "If you give me a shilling Gwyn, I shall go away and stop bothering you". He was a very mischievous lad but it was of course mother who wanted us to keep playing. If it went quiet she thought we were getting up to something! It is amazing how much music we got through on those evenings!

It was at this time that Gwyn decided to take his FTCL and of course I accompanied for the exam which included the Beethoven violin concerto. He passed with flying colours but soon after decided that he would like to change from violin to the viola. He liked the bigger instrument and the mellow sound it made. He also said that he would stand a better chance of getting into an orchestra on viola when he left the army, which was fast approaching so he decided to apply to the Bournemouth Symphony Orchestra for an audition.

The day of the audition arrived and once again I was going to accompany for him. We went to Bournemouth by train from Waterloo and walked from the station to the Winter Gardens, where BSO performed and where the auditions were being held. Gwyn was rather nervous because, although he could play all the pieces brilliantly, he was worried about the sight reading. He had not been playing the viola very long and he confessed that he could still not read the alto clef too well. He was reading the C clef a fifth down from the treble clef rather than automatically reading the music as written.

A poster of the next BSO concert was on one of the billboards we passed and one of the works was the 'St Anthony Variations' by Brahms. Gwyn jokingly said "If I get that for my audition I shall be fine because I was playing 'St Anthony Variations' last week on the alto saxophone". We arrived in plenty of time for the audition and there were a few other people in the waiting room, including Margaret Artus, a left handed viola player. She was offered a trial at that time with BSO but she also did an audition in Birmingham around the same time and was accepted straight away so she naturally took the CBSO job. Gwyn met up with her a few years later when he went to CBSO.

The auditioning door opened and Charles Groves, BSO's Principal Conductor, called out "Gwyn Williams". Gwyn said "I have brought my own accompanist, Mr Groves". He was not aware that Charles Groves was accompanying for the auditions. Subsequently Charles never let me forget how I had ousted him from his position! The pieces went well and I then departed as the sight-reading was to follow. From outside the room I heard – guess what? – the 'St Anthony Variations' being played brilliantly. Needless to say Gwyn passed the audition and was due to start as soon as he finished his National Service.

Gwyn now had a good job paying all of £15 a week and this is when he asked me to marry him. We got engaged in December on my 21st birthday and thought we would marry two years later. My mother was not at all happy about the engagement because she said that Gwyn was taking me away from my music! Little did she know that this was far from the truth. Fortunately Gwyn was by now in Bournemouth with BSO and, after achieving LTCL, I was continuing with my studies for GTCL and LRAM.

There were tensions at home but I just got on with everything until I became ill in June 1961. I was being treated for acute intestinal colic but, after a week, I became very ill and delirious. The Doctor arrived and examined me, and immediately called for an ambulance to take me to hospital. I had peritonitis and had a five-hour operation as soon as I arrived at the hospital. I was very poorly and spent weeks in hospital. Whenever he could Gwyn found time to come from Bournemouth to see me. If my parents were there at the same time as Gwyn there was an atmosphere which raised my temperature. It became necessary for the Doctors to speak to my parents about this situation.

In those days if you had been very ill you were sent to a convalescent home, after being discharged from hospital, and it was decided that this should happen to me. The hospital authorities wanted to send me to a convalescent home run by nuns in Bournemouth but my parents were furious. There was a great furore over this and my parents would not bring my clothes on the day I was due to leave the hospital. I was meant to be taken by ambulance to Bournemouth. However after a strict talking to by the surgeon, this would never happen today, my parents brought my clothes and I departed for Bournemouth.

I was at the convalescent home for three weeks and during that time Gwyn and I decided that we would get married sooner rather than later. We also decided that I would not go home again after leaving the convalescent home but I would go and live with Gwyn's Grandmother who lived in Edmonton. Gwyn's parents were very good to me and the wedding was arranged for August 19th 1961 in St Andrews Church Boscombe, where Gwyn was living at the time. I made my wedding dress with the help of grandma with material bought by Gwyn's parents. The deal was that I should make the dress that Gwyn's mum would wear for the wedding, which I did plus making my going away outfit.

It was Gwyn and his parents who paid for the wedding but it was not a grand affair by any means. Friends and relatives attended, who could keep the secret from my parents. The Registrar of Trinity College, Reginald Batten, offered to give me away but my brother John wanted this job, especially as he had a similar experience at his wedding. As my parents did not know about the wedding they were not present. Neither was my younger brother Dennis, who was only thirteen at the time. We waited with bated breath when the vicar said "if there is any person here present who knows any reason why these two people should not be joined together... etc." We were relieved when there was silence and we continued with the wedding ceremony.

We had a modest wedding breakfast and then departed by train to Weymouth for a week's honeymoon in B&B accommodation. Someone had filled our cases with confetti and we spent most of the night picking up every piece of confetti so that the landlady would not guess we were on honeymoon.

Following the honeymoon we moved back to Boscombe in a rented first floor flat with one room and a kitchen and bathroom shared with the landlady. This was by no means satisfactory but, as I was unable to work following my operation, it was up to Gwyn to pay for everything. After we had been married a few weeks we had a letter from the bank manager in Bexleyheath, where I had my previous bank account. He said that my parents were trying to find me so could I please contact them. Gwyn wrote to my Mum and Dad informing them that we were now married and living in Bournemouth. We then received a congratulations card saying they would like to see us, so eventually went to make our peace with them.

At £15 a week it was not easy to make ends meet and, as Gwyn was paid weekly on a Thursday, by Wednesday we were broke! I remember one Wednesday night we had very little left to eat so I decided to make jam dumplings with the few things I had in the larder. Unfortunately, I must have used too much water because the dumplings started to turn into a gooey disgusting paste. We had to throw them down the sink but unfortunately they started to come up through the bath in the bathroom next to the kitchen. We had to scoop the dumplings out of the bath and flush them down the toilet. It took some time to clear up this mess and we were worried that the landlady would appear at anytime. Fortunately she was out that evening. I have to say that it was many years before I would risk making a dumpling!

Soon after the dumpling incident we decided to look for another flat. We were paying £3.00 a week for the Boscombe flat but we found a very nice attic flat in Winton for £3.50 a week. It was very small and like a scene from La Boheme in the attic, but we were very happy there and enjoyed our Bournemouth days. By this time my health had improved and I applied for a job as Head of Music at a newly opened secondary modern school in Lytchett Minster, Dorset. It was a bit ambitious to apply for a Head of Music post as my first job, but much to my surprise, I got the job and this meant we were both earning and a lot better off.

I enjoyed many BSO concerts in the Winter Gardens with Sir Charles Groves as conductor. When Sir Charles left Bournemouth Constantin Silvestri was appointed principal conductor and these were very exciting times. I remember very well the first concert that Silvestri conducted with BSO in Salisbury Cathedral. 'Tristan and Isolde' was on the programme and I was on the edge of my seat with the deep emotion brought into that work, which I shall never forget.

In 1967 the BSO made its first European tour behind the Iron Curtain. Organised by Victor Hochhauser, this was to East Germany, Poland and Czechoslovakia and there were many experiences, especially as the tour was not well planned, and at times chaotic! It was also all behind the Iron Curtain. In Leipzig the orchestra did not play in the Gewandhaus but in a small hall so they had to give two performances on the same day to cater for the large audience.

After the concert the Gewandhaus orchestra gave a reception for the BSO. When the Gewandhaus orchestra made a return visit to Bournemouth one of the pieces on the programme was Elgar's 'Introduction and Allegro' and the strings doubled up so that the two orchestras were playing together, which was a wonderful experience. After the concert the BSO hosted a reception in one of the hotels for the Germans. This was a seated dinner and the sections of each orchestra were seated together. I remember Gwyn telling me that he asked one of the German viola players what he liked best about England and, looking furtively around him to see that none of the KGB were close at hand, he said "freedom of speech". During their time in Bournemouth the East Germans bought children's clothes in Marks and Spencer's and fruit to take back with them. This was all a great experience for both orchestras.

The BSO was asked to accompany the ballet at the Edinburgh Festival but Kenneth Matchett, the manager of BSO, insisted that in addition, they should also have an orchestral concert conducted by Silvestri, as part of the Festival. This was agreed and the BSO concert, which included Tchaikovsky's Manfred Symphony, made front page news in the papers saying this was arguably the best provincial orchestra in the country.

In 1966 Silvestri recorded with BSO Scheherazade for EMI in the Winter Gardens. The following year Silvestri became a British citizen and frequently programmed British music. He was related to Enesco and he introduced this music to Bournemouth especially the 'Rumanian Rhapsodies'. One of his tricks at the end of the concert, when the audience were wanting an encore, he would leap onto the rostrum and get the orchestra to play just the last bar of a 'Rumanian Rhapsody' and then turn to the audience as if to say "that's your lot". His tragic death in 1969 at the early age of fifty-six shocked the music world. His wife Regina described the BSO partnership with Silvestri as "the sweet magic of a love affair". Gwyn always said how lucky he was to have played under the great Constantin Silvestri with BSO and with the great Sir Simon Rattle in CBSO.

With our two incomes we were saving for our own home at last and we started to look for a suitable house. We found a very nice detached house, one of two houses being built at Stapehill, Wimborne for £3,250. We had just enough for the deposit and could just about manage the mortgage. We were given two armchairs by friends, bought a second hand wardrobe for £3 and Gwyn's parents gave us a fridge and bought us a Formica table and four chairs. We had a cooker on HP and Gwyn decided to buy a bed on HP, which was £80. I said this was an enormous sum to pay for a bed but Gwyn insisted that the bed was very important, so we had the expensive bed!

Because I had married Gwyn, my mother sold the Bluthner piano, which I had been told previously was mine on my 21st birthday, to the Blackheath Conservatoire of Music. Gwyn very generously promised me a piano when we had a home of our own, as he knew how much I missed playing. Mrs Sparham, our formidable but well meaning landlady in Winton lived on the ground floor of the house and would often grab us just as we were ascending the stairs, to say something because she always loved a chat! She knew the situation with the piano and one day collared me as I put my first step on the stairs. She said that her gardener knew an elderly couple in Canford Cliffs who were going into a nursing home. The husband had already gone but the old lady was left at home to sell the house and the beautiful antique furniture they owned. The couple had come from Germany and the gentleman had had lessons from Joachim (the great Hungarian violinist who had worked closely with Brahms) and his wife accompanied for him. They had a Rittmuller grand piano which had come from East Germany. The piano would naturally have to be sold when they moved to the nursing home but they wanted it to go to someone who could play.

In those days I could play rather well so I was invited to the very grand house and greeted by the charming old lady, who in a very cultured voice said "play to me". I played Mozart, Schubert, Brahms etc. Every time I stopped playing she said "play again". After about forty-five minutes of playing she asked us about ourselves and about the new house. She then asked us how much we could afford and we had to confess that we only had £30. She replied in her very grand voice "You can have the piano, the piano stool and the garden roller thrown in to help get your new garden sorted".

As soon as we moved into the house we had the piano. Unfortunately as the piano was situated in a music room on the first floor of the house, we had to find the money to get the piano lifted over the banisters and transported from Canford Cliffs to Wimborne. This cost more than the piano so we had to borrow the money for the removal. However I now had a piano and could start practising again, besides teaching. By this time I had moved to Parkstone Grammar School as Head of Music and I was accompanying not only for Gwyn but also for other instrumentalists in the BSO. I was asked to accompany some BSO brass players for a BBC programme but I was not in the Musicians Union. In those days it was crucial to be in the MU if you were accompanying for MU members, especially for BBC work so reluctantly I joined the MU.

Due to my serious operation we had been told that we should not start a family for two years but by now the two years were up and we decided we would like to start a family. I soon became pregnant but suffered dreadful morning sickness. I heard that a piano teaching practice in Verwood Dorset was vacant. This was in a Mrs Hughes' front room and a number of piano pupils from the village were wanting to carry on lessons following the departure of the previous piano teacher. I discussed my situation with Mrs Hughes and she thought that if I took the position I could teach right up until the birth of baby and then go back soon after the birth and she would look after baby, when I was teaching. This seemed to be a really good arrangement so I decided to give up school teaching and concentrate on piano teaching.

I gave birth the day after I had spent a busy day piano teaching and our beautiful daughter, Julia was born on July 8th 1964 in the Lansdowne Nursing Home, Bournemouth after only 5 hours in labour. We were over the moon with our new baby daughter and Gwyn's parents, who had by now moved to Wimborne were thrilled to have their first grandchild. I continued teaching the piano in Verwood taking Julia with me. Fortunately Mrs Hughes was very pleased to be looking after Julia, when I taught and, as she was a good baby, it was not a problem. I then took on a piano teaching post at Cranborne School. They had mothercraft sessions at the school and, when I arrived to teach, three girls would come to the car to take Julia off with them for the afternoon. They practised on a real baby, which I don't think would be allowed these days but Julia had a wonderful time and looked forward to our school trips.

Gwyn's Bournemouth days brought many memorable concerts but also some nerve racking experiences including one bank holiday weekend when the mods and rockers descended upon Bournemouth on their Harley Davidsons. There was a concert that night in the Winter Gardens and the mods and rockers climbed onto the roof and started to bang as hard as they could. I was pregnant with Julia at the time and terrified but the orchestra played on and eventually the noise subsided. When we came out of the hall all the trouble makers had disappeared due to police having been called.

The BSO principal viola was Cedric Morgan and the leader, when Gwyn started with BSO, was the wonderful Felix Kok – there will be more about him in the next chapter when he went to CBSO as leader. Paavo Berglund followed Silvestri as principal conductor of BSO and there will also be more about him in another chapter.

One BSO occasion I vividly remember was in a performance of 'Messiah'. One of the second violins, who shall remain nameless, caused an incident when he fell asleep and fell off his chair in the performance and had to be carried out on the pretext that he had been taken ill.

Although there were many very exciting times professionally and socially, Gwyn was now thinking of making a move from Bournemouth as rank and file player to a better position. He applied to Birmingham for a sub principal position in the CBSO and was accepted. By this time Felix Kok had become leader of CBSO so he knew Gwyn and his playing very well. Julia was nearly three and we thought it a good time to make a move. There was an economic squeeze during this period and we found it difficult to sell the house. In the end we decided to put our furniture into store and move to a flat in Harborne, Birmingham, so the three of us could be together.

Birmingham and CBSO started another exciting chapter in our lives.

Chapter 4

LIFE IN THE VILLAGE OF WILMCOTE, STRATFORD UPON AVON

Our flat in Harborne was over a butcher's shop, so the butcher became a very kind neighbour and for the six months we were there we had the luxury of good meat whenever we wanted it. We were also near Queen's Park and Julia loved going with me to the park daily on her tricycle.

Gwyn was enjoying his work with the City of Birmingham Symphony Orchestra, and whenever he had free time we looked for suitable properties. We found a road of new bungalows being built in the pretty village of Wilmcote, twenty miles from Birmingham and three miles north of Stratford upon Avon. We managed to sell the house in Wimborne and immediately decided to buy one of the new bungalows in Wilmcote.

We loved the village, where we discovered Mary Arden's House, the beautiful 15th-century birthplace of Mary Arden, Shakespeare's mother, just around the corner. The village had a wonderful community feel, although at first we were looked on rather suspiciously when we went into the local pub 'The Masons Arms'. Having been here now for over 50 happy years we are at last accepted as fellow villagers!

On his days off from the CBSO Gwyn was very lucky to be asked to freelance with the BBC Midland Radio Orchestra based at Pebble Mill, Birmingham. He enjoyed meeting other musicians and playing lighter music. He became great friends with Jim Davis the leader, and his wife Sylvia Knussen, sister of the composer Oliver Knussen and occasionally played chamber music with these fine musicians, together with Harold Rich, piano.

On most Sundays, which were then days off for the CBSO, Gwyn was asked to play for 'The Golden Shot' and 'New Faces' (the forerunner of 'Britain's Got Talent') at the ITV studios in Birmingham. The three-hour rehearsal in the afternoon followed by the live television show turned out to be quite lucrative work, allowing us to buy various things for our new home. We had a 'Golden Shot' carpet and a 'New Faces' TV among other things. Gwyn also took on viola-teaching posts at Worcester Grammar School and then later at King's School Worcester, where he taught the young choristers, many of whom are now notable figures in the music world.

I started piano-teaching from home and found I was teaching piano to most of the village children. I also had pupils from Stratford College including a young Chinese girl from Hong Kong, who was very talented and made great progress. She passed Grade VIII Associated Board with distinction and won a place at the Royal College of Music. Her parents were so delighted that they had a silver cup made in the name of Stephannie Williams as a prize for the piano class of the Hong Kong Music Festival. I felt this was a great honour when I was sent the brochure of the festival with a photograph of the first recipient.

Gwyn and I taught violin and piano to two lovely American girls, Clara and Mary Shaw from Cleveland, Ohio. Their father, a drama lecturer, was on a year's sabbatical from his University and had come to Stratford to study Shakespeare. These two girls were a joy to teach, reaching a very high standard in the year we taught them. Mary married an Englishman and made her home not far from Stratford upon Avon.

I became pregnant again and Julia was very excited about having a new baby in the family. When I was two and half months pregnant I caught the Asian Flu virus of 1967 and was quite ill. What we did not know at the time was that this had a serious effect on the baby. Kathryn was born at home on March 18th 1968 after just two and half hours in labour. She was a beautiful baby and Julia was thrilled that Kathryn had brought with her a gift of a little fluffy ball, which was tucked at the end of her crib. Kathryn was a perfect baby and rarely cried but I soon realised that this was not normal, but more of that later.

Guy and Jane Woolfenden had just moved into the village and Jane and I became firm friends and still are to this day. Guy had recently been appointed Head of Music to the Royal Shakespeare Company and was always busy composing day and night for RSC productions. On one of my visits to the Woolfenden's home Guy had been to Hamley's, the famous toy shop in London, to buy a music box and other toys to work into his music for a production of 'The Winter's Tale'. The music for this was quite ingenious. Guy introduced me to some fascinating work in the theatre.

I was asked to teach the actress Sheila Allen to play Schubert's 'Marche Militaire' on the piano for her role in Strindberg's 'Dance of Death'. Sheila had played the piano as a child up to Associated Board Grade V, but it was quite a challenge to teach her to concert standard in three weeks, so I arranged the music to make it a little easier. It worked well and she played very successfully in the Stratford production, which then went on to the Theatre Royal, Newcastle and finally at the Barbican, London.

Knowing how well Sheila had progressed, the actress Darlene Johnson asked me to teach her the piano. Darlene and her flatmate Ruby Wax were both in productions at Stratford upon Avon at this time and I visited the flat frequently to teach Darlene. One day Darlene and Ruby confided in me that they had written a show called 'The Johnson Wax Floor Show'. They had managed to book The Swan Theatre for a late night performance of their show for fellow-actors and friends. It was a great show (starting at midnight!) by this very talented pair and I was quite taken aback when they asked me if I would represent them for this show. Of course I refused as I had no idea what I could do for them! Many years later when Ruby became a big name my daughters said "Mum, you were stupid to turn them down because, if you had taken them on, you would be a millionaire by now!"

As I knew Jane and Guy so well I was often invited to opening nights at the RST and after performances was taken backstage to meet Judi Dench, Richard Pasco and many others, all starting their acting careers at that time. It is interesting to see how many of these young unknown, but talented actors and actresses later became huge names in the world of the theatre, film and television, including Ralph Fiennes, Sir Derek Jacobi, Sir Ben Kingsley, Barbara Leigh Hunt, Sir Ian McKellen, Dame Helen Mirren, Jonathan Pryce, Sir Simon Russell Beale, Dame Janet Suzman, Josette Simon, Dame Maggie Smith, Sir Patrick Stewart and David Suchet.

Guy was also a fine conductor and conducted the Warwickshire Symphony Orchestra during this period and asked me if I would play the celeste in one of the concerts. I had to play in Kodaly's 'Hary Janos Suite' and in 'Delilah the Delectable Cow' narrated by Johnny Morris. The celeste represented Delilah crying. I was not worried about playing the 'Delilah' piece but I was very worried about the Kodaly, which had 32 bars rest at the beginning of the 'Viennese Musical Clock'. Jane came to the house to go through it with me but I needn't have worried because Guy gave me a very clear indication on my cue. This was my first experience of orchestral playing, and I was so grateful for the opportunity.

I was asked to take a temporary appointment as Head of Music at the Stratford upon Avon High School for boys. By this time Gwyn's parents had moved to Stratford and enjoyed baby-sitting, enabling me to take up this temporary teaching post. My most challenging time was teaching music to 14-year-old skinheads. I knew these boys loved football and found that using a football pitch on the blackboard gave me the opportunity to involve two teams in music quizzes. The boys learned a lot through this, moved on to singing and eventually enjoyed participating in choruses from Gilbert & Sullivan operas.

Gwyn and I had struck up a friendship in the Bournemouth Symphony Orchestra with the leader, Felix Kok, and his pianist wife Ann Steele, and this continued when we all moved to the CBSO. Ann asked me to teach their children the piano, so I often made the trip from Wilmcote to Sutton Coldfield, with my girls, although sometimes Ann would bring their children to me in Wilmcote. Our friendship was such that Ann became Godmother to Kathryn.

The CBSO toured a great deal, so Felix and Gwyn were sometimes away for weeks on end. During these periods Ann would invite me to stay with her – giving the children extra piano lessons, but the company was also good for the girls and myself. Ann had two beautiful Steinway pianos and, when the children were in bed, we enjoyed playing piano duos together.

During this period I was still giving private lessons on the piano at home, but when I gave up the secondary school teaching I voluntarily taught music at the local primary school, where Julia was a pupil, and Kathryn came with me. Richard and Stephen Woolfenden, the latter now a celebrated film and television director, also attended Wilmcote School, where Jane and I put on musical performances with the children for Christmas, with Jane teaching recorder and percussion, and me teaching singing and accompanying these amazing Christmas productions.

I was getting concerned about my baby Kathryn, because she was not responding as other children, although she was very beautiful. I voiced my concerns to my wonderful GP Dr Coigley, who listened to all I had to say and then gave me some books to read on Autism. I returned to him a week later to say I was sure my daughter was autistic – and he replied that as a mother always knows best he would organise a consultation for Kathryn with Dr Ounsted at the Park Hospital for Children in Oxford.

I was very fortunate that Jane Woolfenden and Mary Kemp, a District Nurse in the village, were both a tremendous support to me at this difficult time. I was giving piano lessons to Jane and she would come once a week for her lesson. When the lesson was over she would say "let's have a coffee and a fag". She would then listen to my concerns about Kathryn, which was so good for me as Gwyn was away a great deal on tour with the orchestra. Mary, too, would listen to my problems and having these two great friends was far better than any counsellor.

Kathryn did not speak but she could sing. When I was giving piano lessons Kathryn loved to sit by the side of the piano in her pushchair and she would sing some of the tunes that the pupils played. She loved listening to music and could even sing parts of Brahms' Violin Concerto. However, once she started walking, which was very late, she would pick up and eat anything in sight, so she had to be watched all the time to make sure she was not eating anything that would harm her. One day she opened the fridge, took out a bottle of milk, dropped it on the floor and picked up the glass to eat it. This sort of thing was happening regularly, so she was becoming more and more dangerous to herself.

We had to wait many months before getting to the Oxford hospital by which time I was pregnant again. When we were eventually admitted to the Oxford hospital Julia and I stayed for a week, and then Kathryn stayed on for another two weeks for further tests. After the tests were completed Gwyn and I were called to the hospital and told by Dr Ounsted that Kathryn would never speak, understand properly, or lead a normal life. The conclusion they came to was that the Asian 'flu virus I had caught when I was two and a half months pregnant was when the brain was growing and the virus had stopped that layer of the brain from growing. There were only five known cases in the country at that time from this Asian 'flu virus, so it was exceptionally rare, but after all the tests had been completed they decided that it was conclusive.

It was a shattering blow and I sobbed and sobbed but Dr Ounsted said "I have thrown you to rock bottom and you have to build from here. The parents have to accept the situation before we can do anything for the child". He continued by saying that if Kathryn stayed at home it would be psychologically disastrous for Julia and the new baby, but most of all for Kathryn who needed to go away to an environment where she could reach her full potential. He suggested that we left Kathryn at the hospital and go away for a week with Julia to see how we coped without her. On our return we should make our decision on Kathryn's future.

After much soul-searching we decided that she should go away. We then started scouring the country to find a suitable place for her. We eventually found Sunfield, a Steiner School in Clent, Worcestershire, run by a Dr Geuther, husband of a cellist in the Midland Radio Orchestra, who helped us to find this home. It was very difficult to get the finances from the county to pay for a private Steiner School, but after a great battle with the authorities we eventually succeeded and four-year-old Kathryn started at Sunfield a month before Rachel was born. Many years later Jane Woolfenden said that she was convinced I subsequently succeeded with my agency and management work and became the person I am because of Kathryn. She said that I had to fight for what was right for her and this is what I did in the future with my artists, who became my larger family. Perhaps she was right!

Rachel was born in January 1972. It was a scary quick birth. I awoke with contractions at 5am and as the birth was imminent Julia was taken to our next door neighbour and Gwyn called Mary, who had been a midwife as well as a district nurse, who came immediately and we were in the car by 5.15am on the way to the nursing home in Tiddington. We were approaching traffic lights at red and Mary told Gwyn to skip the traffic lights and put his foot down because she said baby was about to be born. Gwyn went over the traffic lights at red and then put his foot down. Unfortunately a police car was just coming up to the traffic lights and of course they took chase but Mary said "ignore the police, Gwyn, and drive faster". The police car chased us with lights flashing but when we turned into the maternity home they realised what was happening and gave up the chase.

Gwyn banged on the door and asked for a trolley, and at that point Mary came up behind Gwyn and the nurse said "She doesn't look as if she needs a trolley to me". Gwyn replied, "not her, the other one!" I was quickly wheeled into a side room and gave birth immediately at 5.45am. The birth took 45 minutes from start to finish. I vowed never to have another baby because it would only take 20 minutes and I would have to deliver the baby myself!

My friend Jane arrived to visit me at the nursing home with six bottles of Guinness, because she said it was good for my milk. She put it all into the bedside locker and later that day the sister came to get something out of the locker, and all the bottles of Guinness fell out on the floor and I was in big trouble – thank you Jane!

Rachel was definitely overdue because, when she was born her nails were very long and her eyes seemed to be wide open and looking at me, as if to say "about time too". I admit I was worried that something may be wrong with Rachel but Dr Ounsted asked me to take her to see him in Oxford, when she was just a few weeks old. He checked everything and then held her up in the air and said "nothing wrong with this little one", much to our relief.

I started piano-teaching again soon after the birth, and also started to play the organ at the village church of St Andrew's, becoming very involved with village life. I was very lucky that I was able to juggle my work with bringing up a young family, plus visiting Kathryn, who by this time had to move from the Steiner Home because they were finding her too difficult to handle. We eventually found her a place at Chelmsley Hospital, but only by getting a little boy from Chelmsley exchanged to the Steiner home so that a place could be made for her there.

When Rachel was about two I was asked to play spinet and harpsichord with an early music group called The Age of Gold. It was the local Doctor's wife who ran the group and, as she had someone to look after her children, I was able to take Rachel to rehearsals, and she joined the other two children, looked after by their nanny. We performed many concerts but the most exciting one was at Kenwood House in Hampstead, an early music museum. I was able to perform on one of the original harpsichords. I was fortunate that the Royal Shakespeare Theatre had a spinet which was rarely used, so Mike Tubbs, associate music director of the RSC, asked me if I would look after this spinet for the company. This meant I was fortunate enough to be able to practise my early music programmes on this spinet at home.

Back to village life and St Andrew's church. Eventually I started a village choir, after Sunday morning service, with singers ranging in age from Rachel, who was four, to Brigadier Harris aged, eighty-two. Most of the choir turned up after the service just for the practice but there were also quite a few church members in the choir, including the vicar. The choir expanded from a handful to about 50 members with only a few who could read music. Due to the age range and lack of experience besides church music, we rehearsed and performed pop cantatas by Roger Jones, later progressing to works by John Rutter.

When Rachel was five I was asked to lecture on music teaching in schools by Harry Jones, a well-known musician in the Midlands, at St Peter's College in Saltley, Birmingham. It was an enjoyable experience as I had excellent students, though observing the students on teaching practice at various schools in Birmingham was quite an eye-opener, as a few of the children had to be checked for knives before they entered school!

On one occasion I was observing a student from my seat at the back of the class, when I saw a teenage boy, in front of me, produce a catapult to aim at my student. As the seats were made of canvas, and I was wearing fashionable pointed shoes at the time, I kicked the seat of the chair as he was about to shoot the catapult and with a startled shout he dropped it to the floor. He turned, was given a fierce glare by me and fortunately the lesson continued without further incident.

Both the girls had music lessons, Julia playing the piano and violin, and Rachel the piano and harp. Julia later started to learn the cello, which she found far more pleasing to the ear than the violin. However, neither of them was very keen on practising and unfortunately they were at not a particularly musical school. On one occasion Julia was asked to play the violin at school, but insisted on hiding the violin in its case in a bag. Asked by Gwyn why she wanted to do this, her answer was "People will think I am sissy playing the violin", to which Gwyn replied "Do you think I am sissy?" Julia came back with "No I don't, but other people do!"

Rachel started harp lessons with Robert Johnston, principal harpist with the CBSO. She started to play on a little Clarsach harp and, as she was only five Robert taught me at the same time so that I could work with Rachel throughout the week. Later Robert became too busy with the CBSO to come out to give the lessons, so we had to find another teacher. Rachel missed Robert and never made much progress after that with the new teacher. As I had made some progress I was even able to play a small part on the Clarsach harp in The Age of Gold early music group. Julia and Rachel thought there was enough music in the house so they didn't want to add to it. Needless to say neither of the girls continued with their lessons for very long. Julia became Administrator of the Stratford College for Further Education, and Rachel is a personal fitness trainer.

As I had contacts at the Royal Shakespeare Theatre, our choral performances in the church were enhanced and given a terrific boost by musicians from the RST and my students from Saltley. To enable me to conduct the performance Michael Tubbs, the associate music director of the RSC, played the piano and James Jones, also from RSC played percussion. A clarinettist and double-bass player completed the ensemble. Most of the villagers attended these performances and the events are still remembered to this day.

In 1977 I was enlisted to organise the entertainment for the village celebrations for the Queen's Silver Jubilee. There were regular rehearsals in our house with all the young people in the village. We joined Aston Cantlow village for these celebrations and the final night of celebrations were to be held in the Aston Cantlow Village Hall. There was no piano so we hired a vehicle from the Egg Packing Station, which had an hydraulic lift and, with the help of the teenage boys in the village, we transported my grand piano from Wilmcote to Aston Cantlow Village Hall.

All ages participated in this event ranging from the Wilmcote nursery school children as Ken Dodd's 'Diddy Men', teenagers singing a selection from 'The Sound of Music' and performances by members of the youth club. Gwyn and I also performed Monti's 'Czardas' dressed as gypsies, and the evening ended with yours truly performing a Chopin Polonaise.

That weekend the Wilmcote Village held a Gymkhana and a fancy dress competition. As Julia was having horse riding lessons at the time she entered the Gymkhana on her favourite horse 'Lucky' and did very well. Rachel now five, entered the fancy dress competition, much against her wishes. My mother, who was staying with us at the time, decided Rachel should be dressed as Queen Elizabeth II and started to make an elaborate dress. I made a cape of purple satin edged in ermine, which was cotton wool with black paint bits to make the ermine. I also made the Imperial State Crown out of cardboard and jewels plus the ermine trim. To cap it all I made the orb and sceptre, which Rachel had to carry. She hated every minute of the necessary fancy dress procession but was delighted when she won first prize and was rewarded with a huge box of Cadbury's Milk Tray.

After these Silver Jubilee celebrations, the youth of the village wanted to continue singing, so I encouraged them to rehearse for the traditional Christmas carol singing around the village. My elderly neighbours were horrified to see young Hells Angels with crash helmets and on motorbikes turning up to our house on Sunday afternoons, unaware as they were that these young lads were coming to rehearse part-singing of 'Silent Night' and other carols for Christmas. This was very successful, and we were richly rewarded with mince pies and donations for the building of Wilmcote Village Hall which was to be used mainly by the Youth Club. Through a number of fund-raising events the young people managed to raise enough to build a magnificent Village Hall providing a great asset to Wilmcote.

Besides continuing my lecturing at St Peter's College in Saltley (until it closed in 1978 due to government cuts) I also greatly enjoyed part-time teaching at Wolverton School and Balsall Common Primary Schools. Meanwhile Gwyn was playing with the Arioso Quartet, all string players from the CBSO who asked me to manage their concerts schedule. This, together with events for the Elgar Foundation is how my artist management and concert agency began.

Chapter 5

SIR EDWARD ELGAR

In 1978 Saltley teachers' training college closed due to government cuts so I had to decide if I would go back to school-teaching or start something completely different and that is exactly what I did.

Gwyn had become a member of the Arioso String Quartet, which was formed from string players in the CBSO and I started to organise engagements for the Quartet. It was through the Arioso Quartet that I met Anne Soden, who was the events organiser of the Elgar Foundation and promoted many Elgar concerts. She asked me if Arioso would give a concert for the Elgar Foundation, which they willingly did. Many other concerts followed, especially as the Arioso were giving performances of Elgar's string quartet and piano quintet at that time with the brilliant pianist James Walker. One of the Elgar concerts with Arioso and James was given in St John's Smith Square when both the quartet and piano quintet were performed to critical acclaim. The Arioso also performed these two Elgar works at Pebble Mill for BBC Radio 3.

At one stage Anne and I thought we would start an agency called Soden and Williams but, for various reasons, this did not come to anything, especially as Anne was so much involved with Elgar and the Three Choirs Festival, Worcester. We mutually agreed that I would start Stephannie Williams Artists and she would concentrate on her Elgar work, which was so successful. However, Anne and I had always worked well together on events and Anne asked me if I would help with various Elgar concerts and work with her on a choral festival for the Elgar Foundation in London presenting all Elgar's choral works. Anne and I remain great friends to this day and have many happy memories of our joint concerts.

Anne obtained very substantial sponsorship for the Elgar Choral Festival 1980, which was to be held in the Royal Albert Hall and the Royal Festival Hall.

As HRH the Prince of Wales was Patron of the Elgar Foundation he was to attend one of the concerts. Work began in earnest because now the halls were booked it was time to engage the orchestras, conductors and soloists for this huge event.

The first concert was booked for 11 June 1980 in the Royal Albert Hall with the City of Birmingham Symphony Orchestra and City of Birmingham Symphony Chorus conducted by Norman del Mar. This was a performance of 'The Dream of Gerontius' with Dame Janet Baker, who sang the Angel so beautifully. Kenneth Bowen and Michael Rippon were the other excellent soloists.

The second event was 'The Apostles' on 16 June in the Royal Albert Hall with the Royal Philharmonic Orchestra conducted by Dr Donald Hunt, Director of Music at Worcester Cathedral. The Worcester Festival Choral Society and Worcester Cathedral Choir provided the choruses and the soloists were Linda Esther Gray, Anne Collins, Neil Jenkins, John Noble, Christopher Keynes and John Tomlinson.

The third was 'The Kingdom' on 11 July in the Royal Festival Hall. This was with the Royal Philharmonic Orchestra conducted by James Gaddarn (my old singing teacher at Trinity College) with his Croydon Philharmonic Choir providing the choruses and Alfreda Hodgson, Anthony Rolfe Johnson and Michael Rippon among the soloists.

The final concert of the Elgar Festival was on 15 July at The Royal Albert Hall in the presence of HRH the Prince of Wales. The orchestra on this occasion was the Royal Liverpool Philharmonic Orchestra and Royal Liverpool Philharmonic Chorus conducted by the indomitable Sir Charles Groves, who was a great Elgar lover. The programme on this occasion was 'The Light of Life', 'Pomp and Circumstance Number 4' and 'The Spirit of England'. The soloists were Margaret Marshall, Helen Watts, Robin Leggate and John Shirley-Quirk. The whole festival was a great success with packed houses for every concert and raised substantial funds for the Elgar Foundation and the Elgar Birthplace in Lower Broadheath, Worcester.

Anne organised many successful orchestral concerts and recitals for the Elgar Foundation throughout the country. Some of the artists engaged for these occasions were Yehudi Menuhin, Paul Tortelier, John Ogdon, Allegri and Amici Quartets, Stephen Halstead, Colin Horsley, Julian Lloyd Webber, Sir Adrian Boult and The Scholars plus many other distinguished artists.

I remember one of the concerts in Worcester Cathedral when Paul Tortelier was performing the Elgar Cello Concerto with the City of Birmingham Symphony Orchestra and he broke a string at the beginning of the third movement. He very quickly turned to Ulrich Heinen, the principal cellist, grabbed his cello and pushed his into Ulrich's hands. Ulrich passed it to a cellist behind and took his and so it went on down to the back row of the cellos. The unfortunate last cellist ended up with Tortelier's cello with the broken string! As the third movement had just commenced they started the movement again and the concerto continued without further incident. It was a very memorable performance. I was very fortunate to be asked by Anne to help her with a number of these events and I learnt a lot from this very exciting experience and also met many prestigious artists.

Sometime later I was asked to negotiate the contract with publishers David and Charles in Exeter for Wulstan Atkins' book on Sir Edward Elgar, The Elgar-Atkins Friendship. I was by now getting used to negotiating for artists, so Anne thought I would be the best person to handle Wulstan's contract. Wulstan was the godson of the great Sir Edward, and his father Sir Ivor Atkins was the organist of Worcester Cathedral at the time when Sir Edward was composing his great choral works.

Chapter 6

START OF THE CONCERT AGENCY

Working around the CBSO commitments of the musicians, I was obtaining really good engagements for the Arioso Quartet and found I was enjoying entrepreneurial skills, although I didn't realise just how hard it would be, especially juggling family life with my teaching and concert work. Gwyn was a tremendous support and it would not have been possible without having him and the family 100% behind everything I was doing.

My first artist, not counting the Arioso Quartet, was Irish-born Caroline McCausland, who played the guitar and sang a tremendous range of Elizabethan lute songs, folk songs including Spanish, French, Italian and of course Irish folk songs plus other classical songs which she arranged for the guitar.

I heard her sing at a Flower Festival in Henley-in-Arden and thought how talented she was. Caroline was looking for an agent at that time so we both agreed that we should work together and see how we got on. I was thrilled when I obtained an engagement for her on the BBC television programme 'Pebble Mill at One'. This was so successful that Caroline was asked back many times. Caroline was ideal for National Trust and Stately Home concerts and we were getting many of these engagements. She also performed in Festivals and gave a very successful packed-house Wigmore Hall concert.

I did however, have a nasty IRA experience through Caroline but she only heard about this from me very recently. Caroline came from a Northern Irish family who became involved in Irish problems, trying to bring the two sides together in the troubles of the 1960s and 1970s. Her eldest brother Marcus, was Platoon Commander in the Ulster Defence Regiment, Derry Branch, and much respected by Catholics in the Bogside. Both Marcus and Caroline's mother, Lady Margaret McCausland were founder members of the Alliance Party, bringing both sides of the conflict together. Tragically Marcus was murdered by the IRA in March 1972.

It was at the time when parcel bombs were being posted to distinguished personalities that I had a parcel put through the letter-box. It was addressed to Caroline McCausland. It was not the shape of a Cassette or Beta system video, as they were in those days. Gwyn had alarm bells ringing and said "I think this is suspicious". We had a detailed discussion over this and then decided the best thing would be to telephone the police. I gave them the background of Caroline and her family. Without hesitation they immediately told me to put the parcel in the garage and said they would call the Royal Engineers in Tewkesbury.

The army, on hearing the history of the family, thought it necessary to send the bomb disposal unit out from Tewkesbury to Wilmcote. A huge army vehicle arrived with several soldiers and it caused quite a stir in the village. The soldiers evacuated the immediate area and took the package into the garage. By this time the whole street went on alert. After careful inspection they concluded that it was not a bomb and opened the parcel to find not one but two cassettes. Imagine how foolish I felt but I was told that I had done the right thing in the circumstances, bearing in mind the McCausland name and the current trend of postal bombs at that time.

Caroline had three lovely children and her husband was Secretary of the Jockey Club, Simon Weatherby. Very sadly he died of a heart attack at the very early age of 42. Simon's health problems had been a strain on Caroline but she had continued with her singing with the full support of Simon. Soon after his death Caroline decided to train as a McTimoney chiropractic and was very successful at her work. She continued to sing but her engagements were more selective.

It was through Caroline McCausland I met with Richard Baker OBE, the very well-known BBC newsreader and broadcaster. He had great musical knowledge, played the piano and presented, among other programmes, the BBC Promenade concerts and the New Year's Day Concert from Vienna. Through Caroline I was privileged to look after Richard's work for over 30 years. It came about when Caroline was asked to perform at Badminton House with Richard Baker, Martin Muncaster, the flautist Ann Cherry and the pianist Raphael Terroni. I went with Caroline to all her engagements but on this occasion the Arioso Quartet was performing the same day at the National Trust property 'The Vine'. As Gwyn was playing, I told Caroline I could not accompany her to this Badminton House concert. Both concerts went well and Caroline said that Richard Baker wanted her to perform in a concert with him at Fairfield Halls, Croydon.

As I accompanied Caroline to most concerts I went with her to the Fairfield Halls. Once again the other artists were Ann Cherry and Raphael Terroni. Richard was presenting the concert but also acting as narrator and playing piano works and piano duets. I sat in on the afternoon rehearsal and, as I usually did, gave Caroline advice on various aspects of her performance.

In the rehearsal break the artists were queuing for food and apparently Richard asked Caroline "does Steve do all these things for you?" She replied "yes". He said "do you think she would represent me, because I am really fed up with the agent I have at the moment?" Richard then came up to me and asked me to tell him about myself, which I did very briefly.

We returned to the Hall for the rest of the rehearsal and at the end Richard asked the artists to join him for a bow. He looked up and asked me if it was okay. I replied "no it was dreadful". He drew a breath and gave a look that I grew to know over the years!

He asked what was wrong with it and what should they do about it. I said that they should all take the lead from him and bow from the waist together saying "Richard Baker Fairfield Halls" and then rise up together. I learnt about bowing from the Royal Shakespeare Company. Richard said "hum, we'd better try that" which they did. After that, in all the years I knew Richard, he always gave a perfect bow.

I should add that Simon Weatherby was not only Secretary of the Jockey Club but also a scholar and he wrote a programme called 'Where Youth and Pleasure Meet' especially for Richard and Caroline. They performed this work around the country on many occasions.

A few days after the Fairfield Halls concert Richard called me to ask if I would handle a date in Italy with Cathy Berberian for a performance of Walton's 'Facade'. I said I would be delighted to do this but secretly I was terrified, wondering how I would get on with Italian! Fortunately there was someone in the village who could speak Italian so I enlisted her help to translate and I managed to bring about a very successful contract. After that Richard asked me to handle his music engagements and later to handle all his engagements.

Margaret Baker, was a tremendous support to Richard. They say behind every great man there is a woman and Margaret was certainly that woman. Both Richard and Margaret became part of our family. On one occasion, when it was half-term, I was due to meet with Richard at BBC Television Centre to go over his future engagements. As it was half-term I took nine-year-old Rachel with me. She much admired Richard, and one day I saw her stretched out on the floor taking in the news and she remarked "Richard Baker makes the news sound SO interesting!"

It was a joy working for such a clever, kind and considerate man, who was a consummate artist. I would frequently go to the house in Radlett, Hertfordshire to run through engagements, travel and accommodation plus have a discussion on the future engagements he would undertake. Richard Baker was unique and it was difficult to find such an all-round artist in his field, Richard had the great talent of making audiences relax the minute he appeared on the stage, and his voice was like rich dark velvet. Richard sadly passed away in December 2018 and it was an honour to have been his agent/manager and friend for over thirty years.

In the early 80s I had many artists writing to ask if I could represent them but I never wanted to become a large concert agency as I believed in attending most of the concerts in which my artists appeared. I felt that if I took on too many artists it would lose the personal touch and besides, I had the family to consider. Another artist I took on in the early 80s was the brilliant Bulgarian violinist Vanya Milanova. I also started to tour choirs, first Worcester Cathedral Choir and then St George's Chapel Choir, Windsor Castle and later St John's College, Cambridge with Director Christopher Robinson.

As Guy Woolfenden lived in our Wilmcote village and his wife Jane had become a great friend it was natural that I should start to look after Guy's conducting work, which then led to the Royal Shakespeare Company Wind Ensemble. The agency was now building up and it was not easy juggling family life with this growing business but I was very lucky to have so much family support.

I made an appointment to see Edward Smith, Chief Executive of the City of Birmingham Symphony Orchestra, to see if he would engage some of my artists. Ed suggested that I should join BACA, British Association of Concert Agents now IAMA (International Artists Management Association). I needed to be proposed and seconded by members of the association. Fortunately I had met Joeske van Walsum when he booked Richard Baker from me and also Michael Emmerson, agent at the time to James Galway, Henryk Szeryng and many other great artists. Michael had come from Stratford upon Avon and I had taught with his father at The Stratford Boys' High School. Michael proposed me for BACA and Joeske seconded me so I became a full member of the association. I did learn a great deal from the meetings I attended, so this put me on the road to a successful concert agency.

At first I was working from home with a part time secretary, Marjory Clarke who was my backbone, but I also needed help in the house if I were to continue with this work. I still needed to care for the family, cooking and attending school events as Gwyn was often away on tour with the CBSO. Fortunately by this time I had given up all piano teaching and school teaching.

Guy asked me to find a few really good singers that he could audition for the Royal Shakespeare Company production of 'The Tempest' with Derek Jacobi as Prospero. They wanted three really good singers who could act as opposed to actors who could sing, for the role of the three goddesses. I found fifteen singers to send for audition and they chose three who were Teresa Lister, Angela Kazamercuk and Christine Botes. Subsequently Guy said that it was a very good selection of singers I had sent to the audition and I was asked to do this on a number of occasions.

Our company SWA took on the contracts for the three singers at the RST. 'The Tempest' then moved from Stratford upon Avon to Newcastle and then to the Barbican so Marjory and I were kept busy with these contracts. With Richard Baker's work, RST, plus the Royal Shakespeare Company Wind Ensemble, touring choirs and more artists including a young Craig Ogden, just starting out on his career, we were getting very busy and it was becoming difficult to do all the work in one room at home.

When I thought I could not take anything else I was called by Bill Wilkinson, Financial Controller of the Royal Shakespeare Company and asked if I would take on the post of Artistic Director of the Stratford upon Avon Festival. Bill was one of the Stratford Festival Trustees and had just been appointed Chairman of the Festival. This was early in 1983 and I accepted the post but it was then time to move from my home to an office in Stratford. The Festival had a couple of offices on Waterside and we came to an arrangement that the Festival would sublet one of the offices to Marjory and myself for SWA work and I would work in both offices, one with Marjory and in the other I would work with Rita Wright, the Festival Administrator. This worked well and so began the exciting and sometimes traumatic work of the Stratford upon Avon Festival.

Chapter 7

THE STRATFORD UPON AVON FESTIVAL

The Music Festival had started in 1983 but it had made a huge loss. Bill Wilkinson, the financial controller of the Royal Shakespeare Company, plus other trustees together had taken on the responsibility, but it was necessary to make a success of the 1984 Festival if it were to survive. This meant getting good artists on a limited budget, but also making sure tickets were sold.

Rita and I had to work fast because we only had a few months to plan and advertise the Festival. I asked Richard Baker if he, Caroline McCausland (guitar) and Raphael Terroni (piano) would give an event in the Alveston Manor Hotel. This they willingly did for a greatly reduced fee. As Richard was a high profile name at that time we sold out easily for this event. There being four Trust House Forte hotels in the area at that time, we managed to get sponsorship from Trust House Forte, on the condition events took place in their hotels. This worked really well and we produced modest but high quality events in all four of the hotels. We also linked with other events taking place in Stratford at that time so we managed to produce a good Festival and cover all costs.

After the 1984 Festival we asked Richard Baker if he would become President of the Festival, which he willingly agreed to do. This gave the Festival some status and, not only that, Richard helped to get his friends involved. Richard was a trustee of the D'Oyly Carte Opera trust and he asked me if it would be a good idea for him to write a show called Mr Gilbert and Mr Sullivan for the 1985 Festival. I immediately agreed to this and we managed to get The Magic of D'Oyly Carte, with all the well-known Gilbert and Sullivan artists of the time taking part. They included Kenneth Sandford, John Ayldon, Vivian Tierney, Patricia Leonard, Lorraine Daniels, Geoffrey Shovelton and Alistair Donkin.

This warranted a large venue, so we went for The Royal Shakespeare Theatre. In addition we formed the Stratford Festival Orchestra made up of members of the RSC wind band and professional musicians from the area conducted by the ideal person for this, Guy Woolfenden. In addition we had Timothy West playing Mr Gilbert, Peter Jeffrey as Mr D'Oyly Carte and Richard Baker, no mean actor himself, as Mr Sullivan.

This major event needed sponsorship so, as American Express had sponsored one of my choir tours, I approached them for the funds needed and we obtained the necessary sponsorship required.

This was the big event of the Festival that year but we only had a three-hour rehearsal in the RST on the day of the performance to bring the whole thing off. Guy did a fantastic job with the music and all the stage hands at the RST threw themselves into it, producing Victorian stage furniture and wonderful lighting effects. The whole thing was in Victorian costume and the event was a huge success bringing substantial funds for the Festival.

There were many other activities around the town and in other venues, including Acker Bilk, the Coull Quartet, English String Orchestra with Vanya Milanova playing Vivaldi's Four Seasons, Thomas Tallis Chamber Choir and Orchestra. In addition Rita Wright, the Festival administrator, managed to incorporate other events that were taking place in Stratford at that time such as a polo match at Ragley Hall, The Shakespeare Morris and Sword Men of Stratford upon Avon, The Round Table Carnival, Open Golf Tournament, Antiques Fair and so on.

The Festival was a success and washed its face. This warranted more finances for the next year's Festival and more money coming in from the District, County and Town Councils, especially as we were doing so much to promote Stratford upon Avon as a town. Up to now it had majored on William Shakespeare, which of course brought in many tourists to the Town. Rita Wright, was a whizz with the finances and organisation and negotiated with the councils, but I was the artistic side of the Festival and also had to find the necessary sponsorship. I know I must have driven Rita mad at times because she was so meticulous and could not understand how artists could change dates, times, programmes, but this is the nature of an artist! Programmes were changing until just before the programme-book was due to go to print. As Rita was the one who did the pagination for the programme she became very frustrated every time she had to make yet another change.

It was around this time that I was working in my own business with Martini and Rossi on a concert in Sheffield with Kiri Te Kanawa and Roger Vignoles, introduced by Richard Baker. I took the liberty of asking M&R for sponsorship of an event in the Stratford Festival. The sponsorship manager, Tony Beardsmore, not only agreed to sponsor a concert with Stéphane Grappelli for the 1986 Festival but also offered the use of Martini Terrace for our 1986 press launch. Martini Terrace was a wonderful venue at the top of New Zealand House, Piccadilly with a fantastic view all over London. M&R would sponsor the launch by paying totally for the elaborate reception. Media came from the Midlands to attend the launch but this time the London media also attended and the Stratford Festival was now being put onto the map.

The 1986 Festival was looking good with a number of prestigious events planned including Cleo Laine with the John Dankworth Quintet, the Choir of St George's Chapel, Windsor Castle, the Arioso Quartet, the Martin Best Medieval Ensemble, George Melly and John Chilton's Feet Warmers, Fine Arts Brass Ensemble, plus many other local events. The Lord's Taverners Cricket Match with many celebrities, were coming to Stratford for the occasion, such as Robert Powell, Michael Parkinson, David Frost, Bill Tidy, Richard Kershaw, Colin Milburn and Fraser Hines to name but a few. In addition there were folk events, poetry festival recitals and much more.

One of the big concerts in this Festival was of course Stéphane Grappelli 'In Concert' in the Swan Theatre with Alec Dankworth double-bass, Louis Stewart and Martin Taylor guitars. A few days before the event – disaster struck! We had a call from Grappelli's agent to say that he had been taken ill and would not be in a position to come to England and perform. After the initial shock we decided that the first thing to do was to contact our sponsor Martini and Rossi and of course the RST. Tony from M&R was adamant we should not cancel but we should find something else to replace Grappelli! What a task it was with just four days to go. Fortunately RST management said they would go along with this and notify everyone once we had found a replacement.

This was the day of Prince Andrew's wedding and most offices were closed but by the following day we had secured Larry Adler, the spectacular harmonica player and George Chisholm the brilliant trombonist plus Keith Smith with Hefty Jazz. All tickets had been sold for the concert so Rita worked with the RST to notify everyone of the change and offered a refund but we were very pleased few people took this up so we still had a full house. It was my job to sort out all the technical arrangements for this changed event besides continuing with the many events taking place over the next few days.

The big day arrived and it was not disappointing. Larry Adler was not only the world's greatest harmonica player but he was also a great raconteur. The only problem was that, once on the stage, he would not leave and we had a job giving the other musicians their allocated time. We needn't have worried because it turned out to be a great evening with Martini and Rossi, RST and the punters all delighted with the occasion. So much so that Larry was invited back to give a solo performance the following year.

Two years later Stéphane Grappelli, although very frail, honoured us with his presence and, although he had to remain seated to play, he and his trio gave a superb performance and once again The Swan Theatre was packed to capacity. What a lovely man he was and I had great pleasure in taking care of all his needs because he was so appreciative. I felt so privileged to have known this great musician and true gentleman.

Over the next few years the Festival grew with many prestigious events taking place, including the Royal Liverpool Philharmonic Orchestra, Cosmotheka, Nigel Kennedy, Humphrey Lyttelton, the City of Birmingham Symphony Orchestra with Simon Rattle, the Moscow Quartet, Julian Lloyd Webber, Royal Philharmonic Pops Orchestra, the BBC Concert Orchestra with Barry Wordsworth conducting, the Bournemouth Sinfonietta with Roger Norrington, the English String Orchestra with William Boughton, Fine Arts Brass, Jacques Loussier, Dame Janet Baker with Roger Vignoles; plus local performances of poetry, drama, art, folk evenings and an eclectic mix of events including Alan Price, The Wurzels, The Band of the Royal Marines, Midland Youth Jazz Orchestra with Don Lusher, Palm Court tea dances and many more.

At this time I had been asked by Dr Donald Hunt, Director of Music at Worcester Cathedral, if I would engage artists for The Bromsgrove Festival. Donald had been invited to become Artistic Director of The Bromsgrove Festival, and he accepted on the condition that I engaged all the artists. This was agreed by the Festival committee and so, this added to the growing musical activities with which I was now involved.

During the planning of the third Stratford Festival a farmer friend, Tom Mahon, wanted to introduce me to his friend Eric Hurst, a wealthy business man, who lived in a penthouse by the river in Stratford. Eric was engaged to a Russian violinist, Rimma Sushanskaya. Rimma had won the Moscow Violin Competition and the prestigious Ysaye medal, but she was a refusenik from St Petersburg. Rimma left Russia to fly to New York with her family but, being a refusenik she had her violin taken away from her before she left Russia and all the recordings made in the USSR were destroyed.

When Rimma arrived in New York with the family she was the breadwinner and taught violin every hour of the day to keep the family together. On one of Eric's business trips he heard Rimma perform and not only fell in love with her

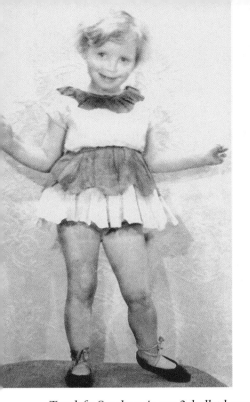

Top left: Stephannie age 3, ballet lessons.
Top right: Brother John Ricketts, Lance Corporal in 1956.
Bottom: Harold Craxton & Dame Myra Hess. Photo taken by the author in 1956.

Top: Wedding of Gwyn & Stephannie in Bournemouth, 19 August 1961.
Bottom: Gwyn with Julia age 8 months.

Top: *First House in Wimborne, Dorset. Called Jupiter (the bringer of jollity).*
Bottom left: *Daughter Rachel Age 4.*
Bottom right: *Rachel aged 5, Julia aged 13.*

Top left: Constantin Silvestri by courtesy of Lyndon Thomas.
Top right: BSO first-ever European tour with David Jones, Gwyn Williams and Brian Johnston.
Bottom: Felix Kok, leader of the Bournemouth Symphony Orchestra and later leader of the City of Birmingham Symphony Orchestra.

Top: *Arioso Quartet in Victoria Square, Birmingham. Gwyn Williams, Viola; Stuart Ford, Violin; Simon Clugston, Cello and Jeremy Ballard, Violin.*
Bottom left: *Caroline McCausland.*
Bottom right: *Stéphane Grappelli.*

Top: Christopher Robinson CVO, CBE, Director of the St George's Chapel Choir on tour in Texas.
Opposite: The Choir of St George's Chapel, Windsor Castle.
Bottom: Choristers of St George's Chapel, Windsor Castle going to a Rodeo in Texas.

Top left: Richard Baker OBE.
Top right: Ju Hee Suh.
Middle: Richard and Margaret Baker in Gibraltar.
Far Right: Rimma Sushanskaya holding her
Stradivarius violin.

playing but also with Rimma herself. When I was introduced to Eric by Tom, he was about to bring Rimma from New York to England and marry her. He was interested in promoting Rimma in the UK and asked if I would help with this. In addition he said he wanted to become involved with the Stratford Festival and become a major sponsor. This of course was a great coup for the Festival and Eric was appointed Chairman. Although Eric and I did not always agree I think we had great respect for each other and this augured well for the Festival. We worked well together as friends and colleagues.

With the help of Eric as Chairman, Rita as an excellent administrator, the other sponsors, support from Stratford District, Town and County Councils plus a good Festival Committee the Festival was thriving. It went from strength to strength, gaining much media coverage, not least from Christopher Morley, chief music critic of the respected *Birmingham Post* and my collaborator on this book, and by 1990 was listed in the *Sunday Times* as the tenth best festival in the country.

The 1990 Nordic Festival, my last as Artistic Director, warrants a chapter of its own, as do some of the Festival highlights, traumas and mishaps during my period of Artistic Director of the Stratford upon Avon Festival.

Chapter 8

FESTIVAL UPS AND DOWNS

I have already mentioned one of the traumas at the Stratford Festival, which was when Stéphane Grappelli became ill and had to cancel. But another event that needed quick thinking was the concert in the Civic Hall with Sandie Shaw. Sandie had been booked for an evening, and her agent had suggested the backing band we should use for this occasion.

The day arrived and Sandie turned up for the rehearsal late afternoon just a little before the band. When the band arrived Sandie handed them the music, only to be told "we don't read music"! We could not understand how we had been landed with this problem as the band had been provided by Sandie's agent but they must have been unaware that they did not read music. What to do now? All tickets had been sold so we had to produce something.

After much discussion we agreed that the band and Sandie start rehearsing together to see what they could salvage from this situation. Sandie sang the songs and the band picked up the tunes and improvised. Rehearsing was still going on when the doors were meant to open at 7pm. We had to delay the concert by half an hour to enable soloist and band to get it all together, which they did, and the concert went ahead without anyone suspecting a problem.

One of the very enjoyable events was the evening in the Royal Shakespeare Theatre given by John Dankworth and Cleo Laine with John's fantastic band. They all arrived around lunchtime, and I met them and took them to the Green Room where food had been arranged. Cleo informed me she was on a diet and had her own very uninteresting box of healthy food. After Cleo had finished her sticks of celery etc., I took her to her dressing-room.

A few things had been requested from the agent such as tea, water and an ironing board with an iron. I said to Cleo "you have an ironing board and iron, but

I would be very happy to iron your dress"; her reply, "oh no, that's not for my dress, that's for John's shirts. I get nervous before a performance so I get dressed in my concert gear and then iron John's shirts – it's therapeutic, you know".

Cleo, John and the band were all so laid back and charming that it was a great pleasure to be with them. The concert that evening in the RST was a great success. The only mishap was Cleo losing one of her shoes as she walked onto the stage. That night we had to have a set that was for a Shakespeare play the previous night, as there was no time for an extensive scene change. It was a very steep rake so Cleo found it difficult to negotiate her very high heeled shoes down the ramp. The shoe came off but she picked it up, limped up to the microphone with one shoe on and the other off. She made a big joke of it all and then replaced her shoe.

Another memorable incident was one of The Bromsgrove Festival events when we had a chamber orchestra performing and the Bulgarian cellist Stefan Popov was performing a Haydn cello concerto. I arrived at the Hall ready for the afternoon rehearsal only to find a very troubled Stefan in the car park. "What's the matter?" I asked. He replied "Stephannie I have left all my clothes at home. My trousers, my coat tails and my what is zis?" pointing to his waist. "You mean cummerbund" I volunteered, "Yes, yes, and my shirt. What am I going to do?"

This needed calmness and quick thinking. Perhaps I could get Gwyn's tails and everything else. I knew Gwyn had a concert in London with CBSO that night but I could not remember if he would be wearing tails or DJ. I calmly told Stefan to go and rehearse and I would sort the problem but secretly thinking what shall I do now! I decided to drive home to Stratford from Bromsgrove and review the situation. On arriving home I dashed to the wardrobe and, sure enough, the tails were there, so I grabbed the tail coat, trousers, a white dress shirt, white bow tie and a cummerbund. Placed them all on the back seat of the car, but not before getting a needle, scissors and black cotton because I knew the trousers would be too long for Stefan.

On arrival back at the Hall in Bromsgrove I found Stefan and told him to try everything on. As I suspected the trousers were too long so I had to pin them up and roughly stitch up the bottom of the trousers to make them fit. It did not matter that the shirt was to big because it would be covered and the tie and cummerbund of course were okay. However, I had not anticipated that Stefan was considerably plumper than Gwyn and the tail coat would not go round him. "How I play my cello with arms so tight?" Stefan said.

Fortunately one of the woodwind players was about the same size as Stefan and he was not in the Haydn concerto, although he was in the overture. We agreed that he would perform in the overture, come off the stage, take his tail coat off and hand it to Stefan, just before he went on stage to play the concerto! Another problem solved but an uncomfortable one for Stefan Popov!

It is not only within Festivals I have had artists' problems but even my husband Gwyn, was prone to vagaries! He always packed his own case for concerts, and, on one occasion he packed my white blouse instead of his dress shirt! He had to wear it of course but he said it was a little tight and it did look a bit feminine! On another occasion he packed one black shoe and one brown shoe. He decided to wear the brown shoe with a black sock over the top. I dread to think what was going through the minds of the audience when he walked onto the stage. He had also been known to take two left feet black shoes and, once again, had to wear two left feet odd shoes for the concert.

Another trick of Gwyn's was to sometimes forget his passport when touring with the orchestra. He would arrive at the airport with case and viola but no passport. This was not too bad if it was Birmingham airport, as I could make a dash in the car from Wilmcote and be at the airport in 30 minutes. It was more of a problem when he arrived at Heathrow without his passport. On that occasion I had the one and half hour drive to Heathrow. Fortunately, the flight was delayed so he had his passport in time, but not without major stress on my part.

As passports can be a problem it is always essential to stress on an artist's concert itinerary – DO NOT FORGET YOUR PASSPORT!

Chapter 9

MY FINAL STRATFORD
FESTIVAL'S NORDIC THEME

1990 was to be my last Stratford Festival, although I did not realise this when I started planning the Festival programme. Having worked so much in Scandinavia prior to this I decided to make it the first Nordic Festival in the UK. A few years later Humphrey Burton, now Sir Humphrey, took up this theme for his Scandinavian Festival in London at the Barbican. This was an obvious thing for Humphrey to do as he was married to Christina, a Swede, and he knew a great deal about Scandinavian music. Humphrey and I have been friends for many years but at that time we were only acquaintances.

My first thought was to visit the Embassies of Denmark, Norway, Sweden, Iceland and Finland. The cultural attaches from all five countries were very excited about the idea and offered to give as much support as they could. The Norwegian Embassy was one of the last I visited and, on meeting the Cultural attaché, Paul Moe, he asked what the other embassies were doing. When I told him he replied "I think we can do better than that!"

By Autumn 1989 I had five Honorary Patrons lined up: His Excellency Mr Rudolph Thorning-Peterson, Ambassador of Denmark; His Excellency Mr Ilkka Pastinen, Ambassador of Finland; His Excellency Mr Helgi Agustsson, Ambassador of Iceland; His Excellency Mr Kjell Eliassen, Ambassador of Norway and His Excellency Mr Leif Leifland, GCVO, Ambassador of Sweden. This was a good start but now it was time to obtain sponsorship in addition to the support from the five Embassies! Approaches were made to Scandinavian companies and sponsorship came from Statoil (UK) Ltd., Scandinavian Seaways in addition to the Stratford hotels, Stratford Council and many other local and national companies.

Performing in this festival was Nigel Kennedy with the London Wasp Factory, a jazz ensemble with the brilliant bass-player, Alec Dankworth, John and Cleo's son. The key element to this concert was Danish, Niels-Henning Ørsted Pedersen, formerly double-bass with Oscar Peterson, and one of the greatest bass-players ever. The Royal Shakespeare Company's Swan Theatre was packed to the gills and most of the audience had come for Nigel, who introduced Niels as "the world's greatest bass-player". Niels walked onto the stage in a smart dinner suit and went straight to the microphone to eloquently introduce the music he was playing. When he started to perform everyone was spellbound and Nigel commented what a privilege it was to perform with this great artist.

The BBC Concert Orchestra conducted by Barry Wordsworth was another highlight with Rimma Sushanskaya, violin and introduced by Angela Rippon. The programme included music by Nielsen, Grieg, Svendsen and Sibelius and was pre-recorded by the BBC for a future concert. The City of Birmingham Symphony Orchestra conducted by Simon Rattle with Kyung-Wha Chung was another highlight, the Nordic theme continuing with Sibelius in the programme. Another special concert was with the Norwegian Chamber Orchestra directed by the late Iona Brown and with Lars Anders Tomter, viola (more of him in another chapter). It goes without saying that Grieg was included in this concert. The Corinthian Orchestra, sadly no longer in existence, gave a Celebrity Concert with Peter Donohoe performing the Grieg Piano Concerto.

The Band of the Royal Marines and Black Dyke Mills Band included Sibelius, Grieg, Alfven and Torstein Aagaard-Nielsen in their concerts. Other artists were brought from the Nordic countries by the Embassies and Foreign Ministries, and they were the chamber group Musica Danica and the Copenhagen Trio both from Denmark performing lesser-known Danish composers such as Kuhlau, Bo Holten and Weyse. Juni Dahr, one of Norway's best actors performed Ibsen's 'Women' in The Swan Theatre. This caused us a few problems as Juni wanted to use a live candle on the stage and the RST said we could only have the candle if we had a fire officer present. This was of course another cost and needed immediate attention to get the fire officer, but we obliged and Juni had her live candle.

Masqualero one of Norway's leading jazz groups, was brought to England for a 'one-off' performance in the Moat House Hotel. Another Norwegian coup was the international trombonist, Christian Lindberg with Julian Jacobson, who gave a spectacular recital in Stratford Town Hall. There was even the UK première brought over from Norway of 'Which Witch' in the Royal Shakespeare Theatre. This was a pop opera coming to Stratford prior to its being taken to the West End.

The wonderful Icelandic bass Kristinn Sigmundsson accompanied by Jonas Ingimundarson gave a recital in the Town Hall and the broadcaster, Magnus Magnusson, having Icelandic parents, presented 'Iceland Saga' in the Shakespeare Centre and gave us a great insight into the mysteries of Iceland. There was also a production of Henrik Ibsen's 'Hedda Gabler' given in the Drama Studio of the College of Further Education by a local drama society.

In addition to all the music events above we were very fortunate to have exhibitions from Norway sponsored by The Royal Norwegian Ministry of Foreign Affairs. These exhibitions included lithographs by Frans Widerberg, photographs of the Stave Churches of Norway and photographs of 'Hedda Gabler' performances through the years.

There were many other things in the festival including food-related events such as the Danish week in the Black Swan Hotel when we exchanged head chefs from Copenhagen's five star D'Angleterre Hotel with the Black Swan's head chef. This was a very successful exchange. Local organisations also became involved and we had what one might call fringe events but they were all included on the festival programme and almost everything had some kind of Nordic content.

The festivities always commenced with a grand carnival promoted by the Stratford Round Table and this particular year the Nordic theme was taken up by many of the floats. The most spectacular was the Viking Ship entered by the *Stratford Herald*. We had made a good start to the festival but the dilemma was... we must end on a high which would involve as many people as possible, and how could we do this?

The mad idea came to mind that we could bring Regia Anglorum to Stratford. Regia Anglorum meet in various parts of the country to present Viking Combat Displays in Viking costume. We thought we could pull together a number of groups from around the country to come and perform on the Bancroft Gardens on the final day of the festival.

By this time I had read up much about Scandinavia and Nordic Sagas. One of the things that stuck in my mind was the story of Viking Kings. When they died they were sent out to sea in a Viking ship and then the Vikings fired flaming arrows to the ship, which caught alight, and the King went to Valhalla from the flaming ship.

I thought a re-enactment of this on the River Avon would make a wonderful end to the Festival. I have a feeling the festival committee thought I was totally mad when I suggested it, but I was undeterred! We had a lovely Norwegian girl, Helene, working for the festival this particular year, and she thought it was a wonderful thing to do. Gwyn, Julia and Rachel went along with this crazy idea, because they knew if I got something into my head I would have to see it through.

The Festival in 1990 was a three-week affair, whereas before it had been only two weeks. This being the case, I thought I would have time to bring the re-enactment about, so I asked Rita to put details of the final event into the Festival programme. Reluctantly she printed in the programme: Saturday 4th August 'Recreation ground – throughout the day Anglo Saxon Viking Battles. Late evening Viking Torchlight Procession through the Town followed by the burning of a Viking ship on the Avon – with firework display.'

How was I going to bring this about? It had been a very busy festival with a great deal of media coverage including Danish Radio taking material for a weekend on Danish Radio. This was to include an interview with me, but the presenter Valdemar Lønsted and his sound technician Peder could not pin me down so eventually they decided to take me in a boat on the Avon to make me concentrate on the interview (as pictured on the front cover).

I was instructed to steer the boat as Valdemar asked the questions and Peder held the microphone. All was going well until Valdemar shouted "look out! You're going into the bank"! With a little help I managed to push the boat from the bank, but I discovered later that all this went out on Danish Radio in the weekend programme!

Now back to my concerns over the final Saturday of the festival. We had booked Nationwide Fireworks for this event but I also discussed with them the possibility of burning a Viking ship using pyrotechnics followed by fireworks and they said this could be done. Now where was I to find my Viking ship? I had heard that there was an elderly gentleman who had a punt, which he took out on the Avon. This gentleman frequented one of the pubs in Stratford so I engineered a meeting and met him in the pub, where I bought him a number of drinks and then asked if I could borrow the punt and build a Viking ship around it, put it on the Avon and then pretend to burn it with pyrotechnics. I assured him it wouldn't really burn and after a few hours of drinking he eventually agreed I could have it for the day. This gave us just one day for building the Viking ship around the punt. How could we do it?

Helene asked for a white bed-sheet, red paint and a paint brush, because she said she could make the sails out of a sheet. This was all very well but we had to make the punt look like a Viking ship and we only had the sails. A brilliant idea came to mind! I paid a visit to the *Stratford Herald* office and asked if they still had the Viking ship they used for the Carnival float. They still had it in the yard but it was in pieces. I said that was fine but could I have it, and the powers-that-be willingly agreed, because they didn't know how to get rid of it! This meant with the help of my two daughters, husband, Helene, a carpenter friend and a few others we could build the ship on the day.

Of course there was now the question of the Viking King. My first thought was, of all things, the RST. As I was quite well known by most of the RSC staff at that time, I got myself taken into the props department and found just what I was looking for. They had a life size model of one of the Henry's who had been in a production. He had been killed and had blood coming from his forehead. I asked if I could borrow this body but I would bring it back, intact, the following Monday. Without too much trouble they agreed that I could borrow the body. I carried this to my car and spread it across from back to the front of the car. I received some very weird looks as I was driving through Stratford and it is surprising I was not followed by a police car. When I arrived home with the body, my family could not believe what they were seeing.

The great day came so it was up early and down to the Avon, to start building the ship. It was amazing what my family and Helene managed to do but we fortunately had a handyman with us and I also went up onto Clopton Bridge to ask a couple of lads if they would like to come and help build a ship in return for sandwiches for lunch. They willingly came to help and by mid-afternoon we had a Viking ship all ready for that evening.

My next job was to go and have a word with Regia Anglorum, battling away on the Recreation Ground, to ask if they would gather at Stratford railway station at 10pm that night. I wanted them to bring their flaming torches and carry King Ragnor (King Henry) aloft through the town to the Bancroft Gardens.

That evening I knew I could not start this extravaganza until the curtain came down in the Theatre. I knew Simon Bowler, the lighting technician and he suggested that he gave me a walkie-talkie and he would also have one. When the curtain came down he would call me from the roof of the Theatre so that I knew I could start the proceedings in another ten minutes, when all the audience would be coming out of the Theatre. This of course meant timing my procession from the Station to the Bancroft Gardens.

I sent Helene to the Station with the body for the Vikings to start their procession chanting with flaming torches and carrying King Ragnor aloft. This worked well and, by the time they reached the Bancroft Gardens they had gathered quite a crowd following and chanting. By this time there were crowds on the Bancroft Gardens.

My next problem was to try and restrain the drunken owner of the punt. He wanted to take it out to the middle of the Avon himself. We managed to calm him down with a few more drinks and then the punt was taken out to the middle of the Avon as planned. Needless to say I didn't contemplate putting King Ragnor in the punt because I thought this was a bit risky, to say the least.

The scene was set. We had the Vikings chanting on the Bank with their flaming torches, Nationwide Fireworks were eagerly awaiting the signal, and the ship was in the middle of the Avon, full of whatever Nationwide had put into it to set it alight with pyrotechnics. It was now almost 10.30pm and I had the call from Simon. Now to wait with bated breath for another 10 minutes. The audience started to drift out of the Theatre and most decided to join the already crowded Bancroft Gardens in anticipation. 10.40 and it was time to go! The signal was given to Nationwide and the Vikings started to fire arrows at the ship. Suddenly the boat was aflame and it was so realistic that I panicked thinking that the punt might burn completely but I was assured by the men from Nationwide that it would be okay. The flames started to die down and a great firework display commenced. What a way to end the festival!

Was it all worth it? We had achieved major media coverage from Denmark, Norway, Sweden, Finland and Iceland so we must have helped that year with Stratford's tourist industry. We also ended up in 1990, listed in *The Times*, as the tenth best festival in the country and that satisfied me.

Chapter 10

WHAT ELSE WAS GOING ON?

During the seven years of working on the Stratford Festival many other things were happening. There was of course a growing family to consider and daughter Kathryn to visit regularly at Chelmsley Hospital. Gwyn was also leading a busy life with the CBSO's growing popularity with Simon Rattle as Artistic Director and Principal Conductor of the orchestra. Thanks to Simon the orchestra had never been so active with foreign tours, recordings, television programmes and so much else. I think at that time the CBSO was one of the busiest and consequentially one of the wealthiest regional orchestras.

Julia was now a teenager and attending the Stratford College of Further Education where, once she left, after a few years working for a solicitor, she ended up as Administrator at the college. Rachel was only eleven when I took on the Stratford Festival. There was of course still the concert agency to run and many other things were happening at this time. As Gwyn was away so much it usually fell upon me to juggle everything such as school events and parents' evenings but between us we seemed to keep all the balls in the air.

When Rachel was on school holidays she came with me to whatever I was doing at that time. On one occasion we visited Lady Anne Scott at Rotherfield Park with Caroline McCausland, who was going to give a concert in the Great Hall. On arrival at this beautiful stately home Rachel wanted to use the loo. It was quite a route march to find the loo but we did eventually find it after having walked through a number of beautiful rooms. Rachel remarked "Is this like Buckingham Palace?" My reply was "not quite". We were then invited to take lunch with Lady Scott. As we sat at the dining table Rachel looked at the array of cutlery set at each place. Lady Scott noticed Rachel's bewilderment and said "I don't know about you Rachel but I'm going to use these first", picking up the outer knife and fork. I thought at that time and the many other times I visited Rotherfield Park what a lovely lady she was.

We also visited Lord and Lady Porchester at Highclere Castle, now famous for Downton Abbey. The Porchesters were friends of Caroline McCausland, as her husband, Simon Weatherby, was Secretary of the Jockey Club of Great Britain. Lord Porchester looked after the Queen's racehorses, so there was a horsey connection. Caroline was due to give a concert at Highclere and on this occasion Caroline, Rachel and I had afternoon tea with the Porchesters to discuss the forthcoming event. It was not only Caroline who performed at Highclere Castle. The Castle was used on other occasions, as a venue for the Newbury Festival, and I remember being there for a concert with the Coull Quartet and also Richard Baker with Lady Walton in a performance of 'Facade'.

Rachel also came to the BBC Television Centre in London, when I had meetings with Richard Baker between his 6pm and 10pm News readings. She found this fascinating but by far her most exciting time was when she came with me for a Pebble Mill at One programme at Birmingham's Pebble Mill studios. During this period I had a number of artists who performed on Pebble Mill at One and I got to know the producer Jonathan Fulford very well. When he moved to London I worked with him on an Omnibus programme with the Choir of St George's Chapel, Windsor. He also introduced me to the 'Proms' producer Ken Corden, but that's another story. Back to why this Pebble Mill Programme was so special for Rachel. It was a significant anniversary programme and many top names had been engaged for this particular occasion. I had Richard Baker performing, but other artists in the programme included the whole of the Hi-de-Hi team, Lulu, and Genesis with Phil Collins. Rachel sat with me throughout the live programme because we were among the invited audience. After the programme there was a reception and Rachel thought it would be good to get a few autographs. Richard started off her sheet of paper with "To Rachel from your uncle Richard Baker". All the other artists followed suit. I think she got autographs from all present but, in later years, the one she treasured the most was "from your uncle Phil Collins" (Genesis)!

Julia also had her highs and lows at Pebble Mill at One. One particular programme stuck in her mind. She saw the Wombles and got their autographs. She then asked Jon Pertwee, who was the current Dr Who. She was very deflated when he refused and said "I don't give autographs to anyone".

Later, Julia had a boyfriend, Jimmy, and she was either out with him, with friends, or baby-sitting with Rachel, if both Gwyn and I had a concert the same evening. She is far more interested in the music profession now than she was in her teenage years.

What else was happening at this time? Richard Baker was a very popular TV personality and enquiries were coming in daily for Richard's engagements, either radio, TV or concert performances. Richard could perform all the works for narrator and orchestra so was in great demand in many different areas. At this time Richard was presenting for BBC the Last Night of the Proms, The New Year's Day concert from Vienna, The Albert Hall Festival of Remembrance and the Leeds Pianoforte Competition, to name but a few of his high profile programmes.

When he presented the finals of the Leeds Pianoforte Competition it was televised live on BBC2. I was invited to the finals of the 1984 Leeds competition and that year Ju Hee Suh, a young 16-year-old South Korean came second in the competition. Fanny Waterman felt she was too young to be pushed into a soloist's world at this very young age and thought she needed a mother figure to look after her. Would you believe she chose me? I had heard her perform the Rachmaninov Second Piano Concerto brilliantly in the finals. The request from Fanny was quite daunting but, when I met Ju Hee Suh and her mother I took to them immediately and decided to take this on.

This started a few years of very exciting times travelling with Ju Hee including a tour of Australia with the Royal Danish Orchestra, conducted by Paavo Berglund. Prior to the tour I had to consider very carefully if I should take on this tour, due to family commitments but Ju Hee said she would only take on the tour if I went too, even though her mother was going to be with her. Gwyn and the girls sat down with me to discuss if it would be possible and the three of them said I had to go as it would be a trip of a lifetime. I booked my tickets and agreed to meet Ju Hee and her mother in Perth, as they would be flying from USA, where they were living at that time.

The great day came and Gwyn, Julia and Rachel took me to the airport for my night flight. I arrived in Perth at about 3am and got a taxi to the hotel. The only problem was that the taxi driver was very friendly and wanted to take me on a tour of Perth, at no charge to myself. All I wanted to do was to get to bed as soon as possible because there was a press conference for the Perth Festival next morning at 10am, which I was due to attend. However I let him take me for a short tour and ended up at the hotel at 4am.

The hotel was beautiful and there were magnificent flowers and a bowl of exotic fruit to greet me. I had some of the fruit and then flopped into bed for a short sleep before arising at 8.30am to prepare for the press conference. I was collected from the hotel and taken to the venue where I was reunited with Ju Hee and her mother, who had arrived two days earlier. I knew that the Artistic Director of the Perth Festival was David Blenkinsop who had been Orchestral

Manager of the Bournemouth Symphony Orchestra when Gwyn was in the orchestra. I didn't think he would remember me but, to my great surprise he came up and greeted me as an old friend.

The tour with the Royal Danish Orchestra took in Perth, Brisbane, Melbourne and Sydney. Over that period I made many Danish friends in the orchestra and friends in Australia. Ju Hee performed Beethoven concertos with the Royal Danish on this tour and became a firm favourite with Paavo Berglund! Paavo and his wife Kirsten also became great friends with me and, whenever Paavo was conducting in Birmingham, Gwyn and I would bring them back to Stratford for a meal.

I have some memories of Paavo that I would like to share. He was a left-handed conductor but also a left-handed violinist and a very fine violinist at that. I heard him practising in the dressing room in Perth and thought "WOW"! After the first concert in Perth we all went back to the hotel for a meal. It was a very fine hotel and the waiters wore white gloves to serve the meal. The meal started with the waiters offering bread. Paavo took one look at it and said "That's not bread – in England they call it Mother's Pride but I call it Mother's Ruin – Pah – I shall get my own bread". He then left the table and returned with his own pumpernickel Finnish bread. He took it to the waiter and said "this is bread". Paavo appeared to be fierce but we saw a very soft side to him on that tour. He was very demanding with the orchestra but he achieved the most amazing results and the Danes loved him. Ju Hee made many return visits to Denmark and Sweden with Paavo, usually conducting.

I had several adventures with Ju Hee in the UK and a number of other countries but we made sure she was not exploited and took great care choosing her engagements. I loved my time with Ju Hee, who insisted on calling Gwyn "Papa Gwyn".

When Ju Hee had her first CBSO concert in the Town Hall, Birmingham, Gwyn kept very quiet and didn't let anyone know that she had been staying with us in Wilmcote. She gave a terrific performance of Rachmaninov's Third Piano Concerto and at the end of the concerto, amid a great ovation, she leapt up and ran straight to Gwyn, sitting at the front of the violas, and gave him a big kiss. The orchestra wanted to know what he had got that they didn't have!

There were many really wonderful concerts with Ju Hee but when she was nineteen she met the love of her life, a Chinese conductor and, after that, she devoted her life to him and his career. She continued to perform under his baton but she never came to England again. Ju Hee married her man and now has a teenage daughter. Gwyn was always Papa Gwyn and Julia and Rachel were more like sisters to her. We are occasionally in touch but I shall never forget the three fantastic years of her music-making.

Edward Smith, the chief executive officer of the CBSO had been a great help when I first started the concert agency, and for many years he booked the CBSO Christmas presenter from me. Some of these comperes included Lord Bernard Miles, Robert Hardy, David Kossoff, Brian Kay, Arthur Lowe and of course Richard Baker.

Meeting Lord Bernard Miles for the first time was quite an experience. I made an appointment at the Mermaid Theatre, where I was told I would find him. When arrived I said I had a 10.30am appointment. The receptionist said "go across that building plot and you will see a caravan and that is Lord Miles' office". With trepidation I knocked on the caravan door and a voice from within said "enter". I did as I was told and saw an elderly lady behind a large desk, knitting.

She told me to take a seat and she would inform Lord Miles that I had arrived. She telephoned through to the next room, and then said "Lord Miles will see you now". With that the door opened and Lord Miles appeared and invited me in. He was charming and also very funny and had a great sense of humour. We discussed the proposed concert in detail and then I departed, making my way from the building site to the field and back to the Mermaid Theatre. That Christmas concert was memorable because he told so many stories adlibbing. The problem was his jokes were somewhat risqué but the orchestra loved them!

The other experience worth mentioning was Arthur Lowe's Christmas concert. He was meant to be narrating 'Tubby the Tuba' with CBSO tuba player Alan 'Jock' Sinclair. Arthur was very worried about this because he didn't read music, so I went to his home in Little Venice in London to go through it all with him. When I arrived he had just said goodbye to the VAT inspector but he was delighted because he had saved all the VAT required to be paid but he did not realise that he also had money due back to him so he was well pleased.

We went through the whole of 'Tubby the Tuba' and he was very happy when I left because he felt quite confident with the work. At the rehearsal for the Christmas concert he appeared rather nervous. I asked if he was okay and he said that he was worried that people wouldn't find him funny. He said "I'm not a funny man you know. It's just that people bounce off me". He needn't have worried because he went down a bomb and everyone loved him.

Rachel was about 10 at this time and took one of her Mr Men books for Arthur to sign. She knew his voice from the Mr Men children's programmes on TV. He was delighted to sign her book and she still has it to this day.

Our girls loved the CBSO Christmas Concerts and it was a time when we could go together to see Gwyn performing, listen to Christmas music and join in singing the carols. This was a big perk of the job and much enjoyed by us all.

Chapter 11

ST GEORGE'S HITS THE USA

My first chapter was about St George's Chapel Choir, Windsor Castle but it was in 1986 I did my first major tour with the choir. We gave concerts in eight states in the USA.

I met Nancy Blair, a really lovely lady from Dallas, Texas. Nancy had been invited to a concert at St George's Chapel and heard the choir sing. She was a fine musician herself and knew an exceptional choir when she heard one, and decided she would like the choir to tour the States. Christopher Robinson, Director of Music, put her in touch with me in 1985. From that time onwards we became firm friends and remained so until she passed away with cancer several years later.

Nancy and I worked very closely together to bring about this mind-blowing tour. Initially sponsorship needed to be raised. We did have a head start because Nancy's husband was President of Hamilton Oil Corporation, which gave £10,000 for starters, a tidy sum in 1986. This was quickly followed by Blackfriars Oil Company. More sponsors followed, including Pan American World Airways, several American hotels, members of Lloyds and Lloyds Brokers, McDonalds who provided meals on the tour and American Express, among a number of other companies.

Before starting on the raising of sponsorship we had to get permission from the powers-that-be in Windsor, so Nancy and I, in trepidation, had a meeting with the Dean of Windsor, the Right Reverend Michael Mann KVCO.

He was a formidable man but he was very fair and had great influence at Windsor Castle, indeed he had great influence over the Royal Family in general. Our meeting went extremely well and the dates were fixed for the tour in April 1986. The one major condition was that, in the contracts, there had to be a clause that, if the choir was required to sing in Windsor Castle it must return to the UK immediately, as Royal funerals almost always took place at Windsor. I think at that time they were thinking of the Queen Mother, but she was fit and well and was only in her eighties at that time!

All was agreed and the sponsorship money was coming in and venues were being lined up. It was not too difficult to get some of the best churches and cathedrals in America because they were delighted to be hosting the Royal Choir, indeed the Queen's Choir from Windsor Castle. We had concerts lined up in Washington Cathedral, Washington DC; the Cathedral of St Philip, Atlanta; St Luke's Methodist Church, Houston; St Mark's Episcopal Church, Shreveport; the First Presbyterian Church, Oklahoma City; St John's Episcopal Cathedral, Denver; the First Congregational Church, Los Angeles and St Thomas' Church, New York City.

A pre-tour concert was organised to take place in St George's Chapel on March 21st 1986. The choir sang that evening to a packed Chapel and performed works that would be presented on the tour. The proceeds from the ticket revenue went towards the tour. It is interesting to note that many of the young men in the choir went on to make their mark in the music profession. Brindley Sherratt is a much sought-after bass and sings in major opera houses around the world. One of the head choristers was nine-year-old Martin Denny who later obtained a masters' degree at Keble College, Oxford. When he was in his twenties he came to work for Stephannie Williams Artists and became a director of the company. He is now Artistic Director of the very successful Windsor Festival.

There was quite a scare a week before the tour because we still had not received the necessary permits and, without these we would not be able to undertake the tour. Knowing that the father of one of the boys had been UK Ambassador in Washington, I decided the best thing would be to pay him a visit to see if he could pull any strings. Sure enough, without further ado he got onto the phone and within a couple of days we acquired all the necessary papers – amazing!

The great day came for our USA departure from Heathrow, which was almost next door to Windsor. We had one young boy who had a nut intolerance so we had to ensure that no nuts were served on this flight, or any of the US flights because this would have had serious consequences for our choirboy. We arrived in Washington DC in the early hours of the morning. It took quite a time to get clearance but eventually we were all on the coach taking sixteen tired young boys, twelve lay clerks, the organ scholar, Director of Music, Head Master of the school, his wife (the Matron) and myself to the hotel. We had excellent accommodation for the adults in all the States, as we had sponsorship attached to the hotels. The boys were accommodated with host families from the various parishes and homes of choirboys from the churches. We had a couple of days to recover before the first concert so everyone was refreshed on the big day in Washington Cathedral. We had not expected to perform in such a vast venue but it was totally full and the choir gave a magnificent performance.

We moved on to Atlanta, Georgia, where we felt we were in 'Gone With The Wind' country and here again we had a very successful concert. Next was Houston, Texas, where once again we had a day free prior to the concert. On the day before the concert we were given a real treat, because the ladies of the church had organised a trip for the whole party to go to a rodeo that evening. When we arrived we were greeted by the ladies who gave everyone a stetson and bandanna to wear for the evening but we were then told we could keep them as a memory of our great evening in Texas. We were taken to a large hall with wooden tables and given a huge beef meal. This was quite a change from our sponsored McDonalds meals! Following the meal we were taken to the arena for the rodeo show with real cowboys! The boys in particular were thrilled with this event and it must have stayed in their minds for many years to come. The concert next evening in the huge Methodist Church was electric. The church was so full that they had to put closed-circuit TV into the large crowded church hall for the overflow.

We then moved on to Shreveport, followed by Oklahoma City. In Oklahoma we had a TV interview lined up for Christopher. I may have mentioned before that Christopher is a brilliant musician, organist and choir master par excellence and I was very fortunate to represent him as a conductor as well as Choral Director. At that time he was Chorusmaster, not only of St George's Chapel Choir but also of Oxford Bach Choir and The City of Birmingham Choir. All these wonderful choirs had the Christopher Robinson glorious sound. However, Christopher would be the first to admit that he was not a good interviewee.

Nancy and I were sitting by the TV in our hotel waiting for the interview to commence. We felt rather pleased with ourselves to think we had brought this about on National TV. There was a terrific build up by the presenter, who was making much of the Royal Choir of Queen Elizabeth II of England. He then turned to Christopher and in an excited voice asked "Why have you chosen to come to little Oklahoma City?" Christopher's reply after a long pause was "I don't really know!" and then silence! It did not go exactly as planned but at least we had national coverage.

The real reason we had gone to Oklahoma City was that Nancy's husband had come from there and, with the sponsorship given by Hamilton Oil, we had to sing in Ed's home city. Of course Christopher may not have been aware of this at the time and possibly could not have even given this as his reply!

In Denver we were taken to the Rocky Mountains, where we encountered snow on the mountains and saw elk at very close quarters. That evening another wonderful concert took place, and then the next day, we moved to amazing Los Angeles, where once again we had a free day before the concert. The unanimous decision was that we should all spend the free day in Disneyland.

Sixteen very excited boys and the adult contingent piled into the coach waiting for us outside the hotel to take us to Disneyland. On arrival, George Hill, the Headmaster of St George's School announced that the boys would be split into groups of four. One group with him, one with Matron (Mrs Hill), one with Dr Robinson and the other with Mrs Williams. George then asked for a show of hands from those who wanted to go with Mrs Williams. At this point I should mention that the boys had seen me in charge and paying for all meals, and so on. After this question all sixteen hands went up. George asked "why do you all want to go with Mrs Williams?" As with one voice the sixteen boys shouted "Mrs Williams has all the money". I was of course allocated my four boys and off we went to enjoy the day. We had a few lay clerks joining us – perhaps they thought they would also do rather well if I had all the money!

Disneyland was magical, and we all had a great time. Later in the afternoon a tired but happy party made their way back to the coach for the journey back to our hotel, where the boys were picked up by the host families. The adults had a good meal and an early night in preparation for the next day, which we knew would be very tiring.

Next day we met in the foyer of the hotel and waited for all the boys to be returned by the host families. It was a short distance from the hotel to the First Congregational Church. We had not expected the reception we received on arrival at the Church. There were huge banners stretched across the grand entrance of the church. The banners had been printed with – The Royal Choir of Queen Elizabeth II of England – St George's Chapel Choir, Windsor Castle. A large gathering was at the church to greet us before the choir went to rehearse for the evening concert. Although all the churches and cathedrals were very large this was by far the biggest.

We were informed that there was an organ at each end of the church and that a special fanfare for two organs had been written for this occasion. After the rehearsal the choir was fed by members of the church and then the choir prepared for the evening concert. Concert time arrived and the choir gathered outside the porch where they had to enter and walk the red carpet down the very long aisle to the altar end of the church, while the specially-written fanfare was being played on the two magnificent organs. The sound was mind blowing.

The choir took their seats and the dignitaries, in ceremonial robes, made speeches, welcoming this very special choir to Los Angeles. Eventually the speeches were over and the choir began to sing. The programme included music by Byrd, Taverner, Tallis, Blow, 'Songs of Springtime' by Moeran, 'Mass in G' by Poulenc and 'Psalm 48' by Elgar. The icing on the cake were the organ solos given by the organ scholar of St George's Chapel, Neil Kelly. He performed 'Sonata No 3 in A' by Mendelssohn and 'Fantasia and Fugue on B.A.C.H.' by Liszt.

This was all an unforgettable experience for the organist, having played on the largest organ Herman Schlicker had ever built, with more than 7,000 pipes, as well as for director Christopher Robinson, the choir and all who attended this incredible evening.

We were now nearing the end of the tour, but we had two free days before the final concert on April 14 in St Thomas's Church, New York. What I did not mention is that all these engagements entailed flights to move from one state to another and we found many of the flights meant changing in Dallas Airport, Texas. We became very familiar with this airport. The boys had great fun marking the pilots so many out of ten for their landings. Ratings ranged from 5-10!

It was good to have a complete day free in New York. Our hotel was excellent but not as grand as the hotel opposite, the Waldorf! It was good to pay a visit to Macy's Superstore and take a ride around New York in a horse and carriage. On this day I was not required to look after the boys so I spent a lovely day in New York with Nancy. In the evening Nancy and I, together with Christopher and some of the lay clerks decided to go to the top of the highest of the twin towers to have a drink in the bar. We all had many memories flooding back in 9/11 when we saw the devastation.

The next day the choir, now quite tired after such an exhausting tour, prepared for the final concert in the very famous St Thomas Church on Fifth Avenue. The programme on this occasion included 'Stabat Mater' by Browne, Five Spirituals from Tippett's 'A Child of our Time', 'Rejoice in The Lamb' by Britten and the 'Mass in G' by Poulenc. Neil played two grand organ solos, the 'Toccata in F' by Bach and 'Sonata No. 3 in A' by Mendelssohn. Once again Christopher with his magnificent choir and Neil excelled and both Nancy and I felt proud to be associated with this choir.

What a memorable tour that was and what a joy to tour with such a professional group, and this included the boys, who could be mischievous when not on duty but, the minute they performed they became totally professional. Christopher was like a mother hen over his boys but the boys and men all respected and admired this great musician, who could produce a unique sound from every choir he directed.

Chapter 12

LAUNCH OF THE MUSIC CRUISES

Many things happened in the 1980s, not least my very first flight! In 1980 I met a French music agent from the company Musilyre, Véronique Réaud, who ran this agency, wanted an English choir to give some concerts in France. She invited me to Paris to discuss a possible tour. I had reached 40 and had never flown in my life, so this would be a first! Since that time I have lost count of the flights I have made throughout the world!

I was to fly from Birmingham airport, only half an hour from Wilmcote. Gwyn and the girls took me to the airport and, after our goodbyes I was on my own. My flight was to Charles de Gaulle airport and I was being met by a lad called Fabian, who worked for Musilyre. I had just settled into my seat when a very pleasant Frenchman took the seat next to me. As my family know only too well, it doesn't take long for me to start up a conversation. I volunteered that this was my first flight. He asked "are you nervous?" "I don't think so" I replied. He then said "I could give you some acupuncture". At this I was quite shocked but he went on to say that he was a Doctor and had been on a convention in Leamington Spa, where it was the best centre in the world for acupuncture.

I naturally declined the offer but we continued chatting until we arrived in Paris and said our goodbyes. After I collected my small suitcase I went through Arrivals and looked for a young lad with a card bearing my name. No one fitted this description so I came out of Arrivals and stood wondering what to do next. There were no mobiles at that time and I had no idea how to use a French phone! My very nice Frenchman appeared and asked me if I had a problem. I explained that I was due to be met by a young lad called Fabian, but he had not appeared. The Frenchman took out a piece of paper and wrote 'Je cherche Fabian' and then pinned it to my coat. I waited for over half an hour and eventually a young lad, with a large red rose, came running up to me and said, "I am Fabian and I am so sorry I am late". All's well that ends well!

My first choir tour of France was with the Worcester Cathedral choir but subsequent tours were with St George's Chapel, because this was the choir I represented.

I was being kept very busy throughout the 80s with family life, choir tours, Richard Baker's work, Ju Hee Suh engagements in the UK and abroad, work for Caroline McCausland, Guy Woolfenden, the Arioso Quartet and then came representation of the Coull Quartet, a very busy Quartet. Here again there were tours and recordings to be organised. The Stratford Festival also took up a large part my time, but, if all this wasn't enough, the P&O Music Cruises started in 1984 and continued to go strong for 35 years. How did this come about?

I was successfully handling all Richard Baker's engagements at this time so all his work was coming to me. Richard Baker was invited to a dinner and happened to be sitting next to Lord Stirling, Chairman of P&O Cruises who asked Richard if he would be interested in hosting a classical music cruise. Besides Margaret, Richard's other two loves were the sea and music. He was still in the Naval Reserve at that time and in World War II he had been on convoy ships to Russia.

Richard jumped at the idea of hosting a music cruise but he said he would only do this if I could engage the artists and organise these cruises. Lord Stirling agreed and he arranged a meeting at Selfridges restaurant when Richard and I would meet the Managing Director, Marketing Manager and Head of Entertainment for P&O Cruises. All was going well until Richard asked "when would you like this music cruise?" Without hesitation they said "this October". Richard and I looked at each other in horror because Richard was really busy for the next few years and we both said that it would be impossible for 1984.

There was great disappointment all round, but then Richard suggested they could get someone else for October that year and he would work around his engagements to enable him to host a music cruise in 1985. This was met with approval but they wanted to know who we could ask to host this first P&O Music Cruise. Richard and I came up with Jack Brymer, a brilliant music broadcaster, who had been Principal Clarinet with the Royal Philharmonic Orchestra under Sir Thomas Beecham, and later in the London Symphony Orchestra. This was agreed, dates were discussed and now my job was to speak to Jack, put together a music team and then work on the programmes.

Dates were fixed, Jack was free and then I had only five months to put together a programme of events. Gwyn had worked with members of Scottish

Baroque and had been invited to tour with them as viola in quartets and quintets for concerts at the Prague Spring Festival and Sofia Festival. This was with Leonard and Richard Friedman and the cellist was Raphael Wallfisch. This seemed to be a good ensemble for our first music cruise with P&O, with the addition of Gwyn as viola. However, Raphael was not free so we engaged the Bulgarian cellist, Stefan Popov. The pianist on the tour of Czechoslovakia and Bulgaria had been Allan Schiller, so he seemed ideal as chamber musician and solo pianist for the cruise. Our second pianist was Jonathan Darlington who, as a chorister at Worcester Cathedral, had had viola lessons with Gwyn. Jonathan went on to become assistant conductor at the Paris Opera and was later Music Director of the Duisburg Philharmonic Orchestra and Vancouver Opera.

We also had a soprano and baritone, and of course Jack Brymer playing clarinet, so there was a wide range of programmes that could be performed throughout the two weeks, which included chamber music, piano, clarinet and song recitals. I should also add that Gwyn was given time off from the CBSO to enable him to undertake the cruise and I was able to get Rachel off school because it was deemed an educational experience. Julia was at the College in Stratford at this time and she too was allowed time off for this trip of a lifetime.

The great day in October arrived and we were to fly to Venice to pick up The Sea Princess. All the music team met at Gatwick Airport and we boarded a Monarch flight with the passengers who had booked on this cruise. On arrival we were taken by boats, which transported us along the Grand Canal to board our ship. Our cases were put precariously piled on other boats. We wondered if we would ever see our cases again!

What a wonderful sight it was when we arrived at The Sea Princess, which was moored beside the Vivaldi Church and just a short walk to St Mark's Square, The Doge's Palace and the Campanile. It was like a dream, because I had travelled very little abroad and of course it was the first time for Julia and Rachel. We were all very tired after the long journey but we enjoyed the delicious dinner served in the dining room before we retired for the night. The four of us were in a comfortable cabin with bunk beds and a porthole.

In the morning we looked out of the porthole and found that we had travelled through the night to the wonderful Greek Island of Ithaca. We had time to go out onto the island for a coffee but then work had to begin. That night we had our first concert with all the artists taking part. We were not in the main International Lounge but in the Princess Theatre, which was the cinema. There was a small stage, which could barely hold a quartet and a white baby grand piano bolted to the floor, but it was positioned so that the pianist's back was to the stage. The acoustics were poor due to carpeting on the floor of the stage but, in spite of the problems, the artists performed well.

Unfortunately the room was over-crowded and we could not get everyone into the cinema! Next morning there was a queue of irate passengers outside the Cruise Director's office saying they had booked for the music and could not get in to hear it. I asked the Cruise Director what we should do about this, his reply "Darling, they were just curious last night but it is Chamber Music tonight so there will not be a problem".

I thought he must know about these things so perhaps it would be okay, but no. The same thing happened with the Chamber Music concert and another queue of irate passengers the next morning. The Cruise Director called me and said "We have a problem so you will have to perform two concerts a night". I told him the artists were not contracted to give two performances a night but I would discuss it with them all. Fortunately they all agreed we should give two concerts each night and this is how it has always been from that time onwards.

On this first cruise we visited Italy, Greek Islands, Sicily, Egypt and Israel. What an amazing trip that was, especially for our girls. When we were in Israel we went on a trip that took in the Garden of Gethsemane. Besides our family, Jack and Joan Brymer plus our baritone took the trip. I should point out the baritone would eat his way through the very extensive menu every evening and Jack would say "My word, he can eat!"

When we arrived at the church in the Garden there was a communion service taking place, and we were surprised that we were given entry to the church. We all crept round the back of the church but, our baritone, wearing shorts, walked up to the altar rail and took Communion. He then got up and walked out, but an aghast Jack said "Good Lord, he will have a taste of anything!" This was just one of the many experiences and to all of us the whole trip was an eye-opener of how people lived in other countries.

I would say that musically it was only a moderate success, and there were a number of problems that needed overcoming. On my return home Richard Baker wanted to know how it had gone. I told him of the various problems and he said that before he took on the cruise the following year we would have to go to the ship and sort the problems. We arranged a time when The Sea Princess was in Southampton and the powers-that-be could be on the ship with us. The Captain also decided to join us.

We went to the Cinema, where the concerts took place, and Richard started the conversation by saying "This stage is too small. You need to remove the front row of seats and then build the stage out". The reply, "we can't possibly do that" Richard came back with "then no music cruise".

At this the P&O representatives decided it could be done. Next Richard said "this carpet on the stage must be taken up". The reply same as before, "we can't possibly do that". Richard came back again with "then no music cruise". Once again this was turned around and it became possible. The next request from Richard was "that piano needs to be unbolted from the floor and brought up onto the stage". The same response from the P&O contingent and Richard's reply "then no music cruise". Eventually everything Richard requested was agreed so a music cruise was planned for the following year.

Chapter 13

RISING STARS OF THE NORTH

In April 1990 the first Festival of Young Nordic Soloists, called Rising Stars of the North, took place at the South Bank Centre in London. Although I had visited the Nordic countries with Ju Hee Suh and with P&O Cruises, this was the first event that Stephannie Williams Artists was asked to promote for Scandinavia. I was busy organising the 1990 Nordic Festival in the summer of 1989 when I had a call from Eric Bach of NOMUS (Nordic Council of Music Conservatoires).

NOMUS was an organisation that promoted young Nordic artists. They chose seven top artists every two years from Denmark, Norway, Sweden, Iceland and Finland. There was a concert organised in Iceland in 1988 for the seven chosen artists that year and then NOMUS decided these artists should have exposure in London in 1990. Eric Bach was a Dane, the head of NOMUS, and he decided he wanted me to manage this event. This was another challenge but one I relished. The first preferred venue was the Wigmore Hall, but we then settled for the Purcell Room on the South Bank. The dates were fixed for Saturday 21 April – Monday 23 April inclusive.

The artists chosen for this London debut were Áshildur Haraldsdóttir, flautist from Iceland; Jan-Erik Gustafsson, cellist from Finland; Dan Laurin, recorder; Olle Persson, baritone and Anders Kilström, piano from Sweden; Michaela Fukačová, cello from Denmark and to complete the line-up Leif Ove Andsnes, piano from Norway. I had engaged the highly renowned accompanist, Geoffrey Pratley to play for the instrumentalists.

As Richard Baker and I worked well together he became honorary president of the festival and presented the concerts. The Swedish opera singer Kerstin Meyer made a special guest appearance on the Sunday, 22 April, co-introducing the three Swedish artists with Richard Baker. All the concerts and interviews were recorded by BBC Radio 3 and by Danish Radio for later transmission throughout Scandinavia and also by Swedish Radio for broadcasting live via satellite.

The programmes included works by Bach, Beethoven, Chopin, Dvořák, Fauré, Janáček, Schumann and Shostakovich plus Nordic composers Andriessen, Sandström, Sibelius, Sjögren and Sveinsson and a contemporary composition by the young Japanese composer Kikuko Matsumoto.

Sponsorship was obtained from a number of companies, including the Scandic Crown Hotel in London, who accommodated all the artists and hosted a reception at the end of the Festival. As I had persuaded the Ambassadors of all five Nordic companies to be Patrons of the 1990 Stratford Festival, I thought it would be a good idea also to get them to be Patrons of 'Rising Stars of the North'. They all willingly agreed as they wanted to help the careers of these talented young musicians.

The Festival was intended to promote the individual careers of the seven soloists, as well as providing a feast of classical and contemporary music. 'Rising Stars of the North' was a rare opportunity to appreciate the strength, diversity and creativity of young talent emerging from the Nordic countries. All seven young artists went on to pursue a successful music career. Press and promoters attended the concerts and Simon Foster, then Managing Director of Virgin Records, signed up Leif Ove Andsnes for a recording contract straight after his performance. Leif is now one of today's leading concert pianists. There were excellent reviews from *The Guardian, The Independent* and *The Times.*

This event established my credentials in Scandinavia and subsequently in the 1990s Stephannie Williams Artists Ltd (SWA) managed many events for Nordic artists. The first of these after the Festival was the Trondheim Soloists, which we toured many times, their first tour of the UK being in 1991. It was just after they had had a great success with the recording of Vivaldi's 'Four Seasons' with Anne-Sophie Mutter. This first tour took in Kings College Chapel, Cambridge; Merton College, Oxford; St Martin in the Fields and Holy Trinity Church, Stratford upon Avon, and subsequent tours included concerts at prestigious festivals and The Wigmore Hall.

The Norwegian Youth Chamber Orchestra toured with us in 1993, conducted by Christian Eggen with soloists Lars Anders Tomter (viola) and Henning Kraggerud (violin). The Fairfield Halls Croydon and Symphony Hall Birmingham were two of the special venues on this very well supported tour.

It was after this tour that Stephannie Williams Artists Ltd. took on representation of the Norwegian giant of the viola, Lars Anders Tomter. He performed many wonderful UK concerts but some of the highlights were the BBC

Proms (in which he performed the Britten Concerto for Violin and Viola, where he was joined by violinist Tasmin Little and the Royal Philharmonic Orchestra, Daniele Gatti conducting), soloist with the City of Birmingham Orchestra, Scottish Chamber Orchestra and a brilliant performance of the Walton Viola Concerto with the English Philharmonic Orchestra at the Oldham Festival.

In 1993 Stephannie Williams Artists Ltd. managed concerts with Icelandic artists. One was at St James's Piccadilly with Sigrún Eðvaldsdóttir and Mark Bebbington. Sigrún is now concertmaster of the Iceland Symphony Orchestra and Mark Bebbington is a busy concert pianist in the UK and abroad. The second Icelandic concert was in 1993 at the Wigmore Hall with the Icelandic baritone, Sigurður Bragason and Hjalmar Sighvatsson, piano. This was followed the next year promoting a successful Wigmore Hall concert with Gunnar Kvaran, principal cellist with the Iceland Symphony Orchestra.

We were proud to bring the distinguished Italian pianist Aldo Ciccolini to England in 1993 for concerts at the French Institute in London, St Johns, Smith Square, London and to Symphony Hall, Birmingham broadcast by BBC Radio 3 and receiving critical acclaim. Other notable Nordic concerts around this time were a Wigmore Hall Recital with Lars Anders Tomter, viola and Håvard Gimse, piano from Norway and Morten Zeuten, cello and Amalie Malling piano.

Other important family events in the 1990s were the marriages of both Julia and Rachel. Julia was married on 10 July 1993 and Rachel on 28 June 1997, which were of course big occasions for us. Being parents of the brides, Gwyn and I were very much involved with the organising. This was very important to us and events had to work around the weddings. They were both beautiful occasions but it is unfortunate neither of the marriages lasted, especially as they had seen their parents so happily married. Perhaps no one could ever come up to their father whom they both adored. However the marriages produced seven beautiful grandchildren, so we were very blessed. There will be more of grandchildren later.

The number of cruises was growing each year and more of these in another chapter, but the most significant thing that happened to me in 1990 was becoming the UK Artistic Director of the William Walton Trust, and this started another exciting chapter in our lives.

Chapter 14

MEETING LADY WALTON

Early in 1990 Richard Baker was asked to give a performance in Malta for Denby Richards, then the editor of the magazine *Musical Opinion* (the editor of the magazine now is Robert Matthew-Walker, a good friend and colleague). At that time Denby ran the Malta Festival and knowing we represented Richard, he called me to see if Richard would be free and willing to perform Walton's 'Facade' with Lady Susana Walton. He was free and was interested, so all was organised.

On his return I called Richard to ask how it went. He said "actually it went well, although I did not expect Lady Walton to be up to it because she doesn't read music". He then went on to say "I'm sorry Steve, but she asked me who looked after my work, as she wants to be represented for 'Facade' performances, and I gave her your number". I groaned because I had heard she could be difficult.

No sooner had I put the phone down from Richard, I had a call from Lady Walton. "Could you come to the Savoy for lunch one day this week as I would like to be represented for 'Facade' and I understand you are good". Reluctantly I agreed to go. Lady Walton kept a suite at the Savoy whenever she visited London from her home on the Isle of Ischia, in the Bay of Naples.

On arrival at the Savoy I was taken to her suite. I liked her very much as soon as I met her and it was easy to make conversation, even though I was expecting linguistic difficulties, she being Argentinian. However her voice was articulate and better than some English people. She said William would have been shocked at the idea of her performing 'Facade', as he only married her because she knew nothing about music!

After some discussion I agreed to represent her, but I said that I thought she would need someone to help her with presentation, having already discussed this with Richard. At this she froze, a look I was to encounter many times over the next twelve years, "What do you mean?" she asked in a cold voice. "I mean that you need some coaching from someone who knows how to use the voice". Her reply, "who do you suggest?" I suggested Cicely Berry from the Royal Shakespeare Company, the best voice coach in the country. Her tone softened and she asked if I could line up sessions for her, which I did.

Soon after this Susana recorded 'Facade' with Richard Baker for Chandos, who were recording all the Walton works. This was with members of the City of London Sinfonia conducted by the late Richard Hickox. I started to organise a number of very successful 'Facade' performances with Lady Walton and Richard Baker, mainly with English Serenata, an ensemble directed by Gabrielle Byam-Grounds and conducted by Guy Woolfenden. Susana Walton, as she was named as an artist, had improved tremendously after her coaching with Cicely Berry and, in addition, I went through it musically with her. I think, in spite of a few timings here and there, she was one of the best speakers in 'Facade' and was a wonderful partner with Richard. She was very theatrical in performance and Richard played it very straight, which worked beautifully.

Thanks to the success of these performances Susana decided that she would like to perform it in London to promote the Chandos recording. She asked me to manage the event, so I booked the Queen Elizabeth Hall at the South Bank. The first half of the programme would be 'Facade' with Susana and Richard as speakers, Richard Hickox conducting members of the City of London Sinfonia. The second half would be Walton songs with Graham Johnson accompanying the singers.

The great day came and the concert was totally sold out. I was naturally attending the 'Facade' afternoon rehearsal. Susana arrived wearing a beautiful hat with a large brim. The rehearsal started with her wearing the hat because she said she would wear it for the performance. She looked at me seated in the hall and said "what do you think of the hat?" I replied "It is a beautiful hat but not suitable for the performance". She looked furious and everyone on the stage froze "why not?" she retorted. My answer was "It is hiding your eyes and most of your face is in darkness". Angrily she said "well they must put lights on my face". I shrugged and said no more and the rehearsal started.

After a few minutes Susana took the hat off and placed it on the piano. She looked at me and said "If you don't like the hat I won't wear the hat". That evening she arrived in a full 1920s outfit with a fascinator completely off the face.

The concert was a huge success and a great many CDs of 'Facade' were sold. There were more celebrities in the audience than on the stage including Lords and Ladies, well-known musicians and even Barry Humphries. I think they were all curious to know how this larger-than-life widow of Sir William would take to performing on the stage. I think they were all very pleasantly surprised at her stunning performance.

I should mention that Susana had a wonderful array of headwear for her 'Facade' performances, but they were always off the face. Her 1920s dresses were made by Mariano Fortuny, the fashion designer from Spain. She also wore beautiful Italian shoes to go with the dresses. The jewellery she wore was always very extravagant large pieces and she wore huge rings, some of which had been given to her by Dame Edith Sitwell. Edith was very eccentric and I think Susana wanted to emulate her. One day she asked me if I thought she was eccentric enough to which I replied "I definitely think you are". She was very pleased with this remark.

Whenever Susana had 'Facade' performances I travelled with her most of the time whether it was in the UK or abroad but I also had the festival and music cruises to think about at this stage, which did not go down well with her. However, the same year I took on representation of Lady Walton I decided to resign from my post as Artistic Director of the Stratford upon Avon Festival. I resigned on 1st November 1990 and on 4th November I had a call from Susana, which was not unusual but, on this occasion she asked if I could get to the Savoy Hotel in London the next day to meet the Trustees of the William Walton Trust. I agreed to go, wondering what this was all about.

On arrival at the Savoy I made my way to Lady Walton's suite. By this time the reception staff of the Savoy knew me well so I did not need taking to the suite. On arrival I was introduced to the trustees and they started to fire questions at me. This went on for about an hour and then Lady Walton said "well you've got the job". I said "what job?" and she came back with "Artistic Director of the William Walton Trust, of course". One of the trustees said that this would be dependent upon three written references. I was very fortunate to get three good referees in Edward Smith, Chief Executive of the CBSO, William Wilkinson, Financial Controller of the Royal Shakespeare Company, and Richard Baker OBE. This was on 5th November, which I remember well because it was Guy Fawkes night. Terms were discussed, and depending upon the references my pay would be backdated from 1st November. It meant I ended my work with the Stratford Festival and started work with the William Walton Trust, all on the same day. How lucky was that.

Chapter 15

WILLIAM WALTON

On that special meeting day I did ask if the trustees could tell me what they were expecting from this new and first-time appointment they had made. One thing was to promote the music of Sir William Walton. Some of his music was played frequently, such as the Coronation Marches 'Crown Imperial' and 'Orb and Sceptre', but his chamber music especially, concertos, symphonies, film music and songs were not performed as much as the Trust would like them to be and this would mean working closely with Walton's publisher, Oxford University Press with Andrew Potter and the brilliant Simon Wright, with whom I am still in touch.

The other important thing, as far as Lady Walton was concerned, was to get the opera 'Troilus and Cressida' performed by a leading opera company and make a success of it. This work was written by William for Lady Walton and dedicated to her, so it meant a great deal to her and, up until now, it had never been a critical triumph.

At that point I thought to myself what have I let myself in for! They had said I had to create the job but now they were giving me huge targets to fulfil, especially as far as 'Troilus and Cressida' was concerned. However, it was another great challenge and I enjoyed greatly the twelve years I was working with Lady Walton and for the William Walton Trust, especially, not knowing at that time, it was to take me up to the centenary of his birth.

With this job came the honour of working very closely with Lady Walton as well as the trustees, which over the years included Sir Robert Armstrong, Lord Palumbo, Sir John Tooley, Humphrey Burton, Sir Simon Rattle, Richard Hickox, Lord Bridges, Christopher Palmer, Jonathan Stone, the Hon Paul Zuckerman, John Camacho, among others. Susana, as I then came to know her, decided that I should go to her home in Ischia to work with her and learn more about the life of

William Walton. In the spring following my appointment Gwyn had a week off from CBSO commitments, so it was decided we should visit together the house and gardens at La Mortella, for a week during this period.

The gardens at La Mortella are open to the public and the house and gardens are very special. The Waltons had the house built into the volcanic rock and it is unique. When the Waltons moved into the house there was a huge area of land surrounding it but that's all it was, and a garden needed to be built.

Susana loves gardens, and William told her "When I am composing you can get on with building a garden". Shortly after this their friend Russell Page, one of the greatest landscape gardeners of the day, visited the couple and said "I shall design the garden for you". Susana replied "but we can't afford you!" His answer was "you can pay me when the garden is finished" but of course he made sure the garden was never finished, so they never did pay him!

We were very excited about our first trip to Ischia. We got a flight from Birmingham to Naples and found Susana Walton waiting for us at the airport. She hustled us to the Aliscafo boat which would take us to the port at Forio, where she had her car waiting. We bundled into the little Fiat with our suitcase and started the very hairy drive to La Mortella.

Susana was not the best of drivers, to say the least and like most Italian drivers, tooted her horn all the way to the house, so we were relieved when we eventually arrived. The electronic gates were opened and we drove through the most amazing gardens. It was just like driving into a wonderland. On arrival at the beautiful house we were taken to our bedroom. Susana said "I have given you Vivien and Larry's suite". How grand and special it was to be sleeping in the same bed as Vivien Leigh and Laurence Olivier had done in the past!

The next day, after an early breakfast Susana and I started working on the veranda and Gwyn asked if he could go up to the swimming pool, which was a magnificent pool situated high above the house, complete with changing rooms. Susana said "of course darling, take the funicular up to the pool and you will find three pairs of swimming trunks in the changing rooms. You can have either Willie's, Larry's or André's". Gwyn could not believe that he was being offered the trunks of William Walton, Laurence Olivier or André Previn! He thanked her but said he had brought his own, although I don't think anyone would be excited to wear his if he had left them in the changing room!

Susana and I discussed all the exciting projects planned for the future. She then took us round the magnificent gardens and told us of the origins and countries of the plants. There were a number of ponds, and one in particular had terrapins and I discovered Susana was very fond of terrapins and spoke to them every day. There was another pond, which Russell Page had made into a figure of eight for William's eightieth birthday. We were taken up to the top level of the gardens where there was a pool with rare Amazonian water lilies. Susana informed us that this water lily changed sex over night. It was white one day and then it changed to pink and after that it died of shock!

The most moving place in the garden was The Rock. William wanted his ashes overlooking the Bay of Naples. You could see where the top of the rock had been removed to place the ashes. There was an epitaph to William on the side of the rock and Susana had written her own for the other side. She said her ashes would join William's, so that is where they are now.

The following day we were taken on a surprise trip to Capri by Susana. We were taken by boat and then up the funicular to Anacapri, where we climbed up the Tiberius mountain. It was a long steep walk but Susana told Gwyn he would get a beer at the top. Unfortunately, the bar was closed when we got to the top, but the views were memorable. After this we were taken to the Blue Grotto and then to the home of Axel Munthe. We also had Gracie Fields' house pointed out to us and were told the story of William's meeting with Gracie Fields. What a special week that was; I learnt much about William Walton and returned home with Gwyn feeling far better equipped to tackle the big job I had ahead of me.

I started in earnest to promote the music of William Walton, besides promoting performances of 'Facade', in addition to working on the P&O Cruises Music Festivals at Sea, Richard Baker's work and representation of our artists.

Susana and Richard had a 'Facade' performance at Longleat House with English Serenata conducted by Guy Woolfenden. This event was sponsored by PowerGen, and Ed Wallis, the Managing Director was rather taken with Susana and with Walton's music. A follow-up at the Coventry office resulted in a seven-year sponsorship deal with PowerGen at £50,000 a year. This needed to be attached to education, and I was very pleased to start education work with major orchestras such as the CBSO, RLPO and also with the BBC for children's programmes.

I visited Festivals, orchestral management and many organisations to promote Walton and worked closely with Simon Wright of Oxford University Press. After William's death Susana launched masterclasses at La Mortella for young opera singers who were starting out on their careers. Catherine Wilson and Leonard Hancock organised auditions in London to decide each year the young singers who would take part.

Colin Graham, Director of St Louis opera house started these masterclasses with Martin Isepp as pianist. Though my work was mainly in the UK I was able to attend a couple of these masterclasses: Colin's production of Rossini's 'Cenerentola' and also Jonathan Miller's production of Walton's 'The Bear'.

Sue Graham-Dixon organised the UK press to attend these masterclasses. One of the press contacts was Christopher Morley, Chief Music Critic of the *Birmingham Post*, and my collaborator on this book. Sue and I worked well together and we received many glowing reviews on the masterclasses as well as on other Walton performances. Sue became a close friend and I was very sad when she passed away a few years ago.

With many Walton events taking place, 'Facade' performances, plus all the other work with artists and festivals the 1990s were a very busy time. With the two girls now married the next exciting event was the birth of Dan, our first grandchild.

It was unfortunate that I was at the Brighton Festival for a performance of 'Facade' the night Daniel William was born. Gwyn was with me in Brighton so the following day we were up with the lark and driving straight back to Warwick Hospital to see Julia and our precious first grandson.

Bulgaria

A couple of exciting events took place in Bulgaria. One of these was the first-ever performance in Bulgaria of the Walton Violin Concerto with Vanya Milanova, the wonderful violinist we represented. This was to take place at the Ruse Festival, and Susana and I planned to be present at this performance.

We flew to Sofia two days before the event and were met by two Bulgarians in a battered old van that had a broken window stuck together with sellotape. It was late at night and we were told we would have a long drive to Ruse. Susana asked several times where we were staying but we were told "just wait and see". Susana was getting rather irritated by this but we managed to have a short nap on the way between Susana telling me fascinating stories of her life with William. We eventually arrived at around 3am and when we got out of the van we found we were outside a very grand dacha with a red carpet laid from the front door along the drive to the gate.

There was a lady, who spoke no English, waiting for us. She showed us to our large, old-fashioned but very grand bedrooms, both en suite. In the centre of each bathroom was a huge wrought iron bath! We were given something to eat and then told that the lady would arrive the next morning to prepare breakfast. At that they all left us alone in this grand dacha.

The next morning, when we awoke in our respective rooms, sure enough, the Bulgarian lady had arrived and prepared our breakfast. A little later the two people who had collected us from Sofia airport arrived and said they were taking us for a television interview! We arrived at a large hall and, on entering the hall, we found once again a red carpet had been laid from the back of the hall all the way to the interview set at the front. Every seat in the hall had been taken and everyone rose as we entered the hall. Perhaps Susana was used to this treatment but I wasn't, and for a few minutes I knew how royalty felt!

After we had sat down we were told that we would be fitted with translation equipment because the interview was going out live nationally. This didn't seem to worry Susana but I was rather apprehensive. The interview lasted an hour and both Susana and I contributed to this TV broadcast, which was not as daunting as I had at first imagined.

Susana and I were hosted royally and taken around the city of Ruse, which was just recovering from the communist regime. We had cucumber at every meal; sometimes fried, sometimes boiled and sometimes just cold but we were given very good Bulgarian wine to drink at every meal so the cucumber was washed down well.

The great event arrived the following evening and we were collected and taken to a very good concert hall. The excellent festival orchestra accompanied Vanya and she gave a magnificent performance, which was very well received by the capacity audience, and Susana was acknowledged as the composer's widow. The British Ambassador had been driven from Sofia to Ruse for the occasion and gave a reception after the performance.

The Ambassador decided it was too far for us to drive back to Sofia for the flight home and therefore arranged for us to drive from Ruse to Bucharest in Romania, as Ruse was very close to the border. We were driven in the Ambassador's limousine complete with flag on front of the car and an escort from the Embassy to take us. On arrival at the border our escort took our passports to have them checked but told us to stay in the car as it could be quite dangerous. The escort seemed to bypass the queue and quickly returned to the car where we all drove from Bulgaria, through no man's land into Romania. At the airport there were armed guards everywhere so it was quite scary and we were pleased when we were on the flight returning to Heathrow. It had been quite an experience but we both agreed it was all worthwhile.

As the Violin Concerto was such a triumph in Bulgaria we were asked to return the following year for a performance of 'Facade' and the chamber music version of 'Henry V', in the arrangement by Edward Watson, composer and clarinettist with the Royal Shakespeare Theatre. It was to be with members of the Ruse Festival orchestra conducted by Guy Woolfenden. Lady Walton and John Amis (as Richard Baker was not free), were the speakers in 'Facade' and one of Bulgaria's leading actors was to narrate 'Henry V' in Bulgarian. I arranged with

Oxford University Press to have all the music sent to the Ruse orchestra, because the hire costs would be extortionate for Bulgaria at that time.

On this occasion the Embassy organised everything for us, so we all flew to Sofia and spent the night in the Ambassador's residence and were driven to Ruse the following day. Once again the hall was completely full but, on this occasion, with mainly young people. We discovered that the actor, Yossif Sarchadjiev, was very popular in Bulgaria, and Shakespeare was also popular with the young.

'Facade' was first in the programme and of course spoken in English but there was a Bulgarian translation in the programme. 'Facade' had rather a cool reception from this young audience but 'Henry V' was a great success and received a standing ovation. All in all Bulgaria was an unforgettable experience for Guy, his wife Jane, who was also present, John Amis, Susana and myself.

I do have another 'Henry V' story, she blushes.

Marjory and I were preparing for a Walton concert of the Shakespeare scenario of 'Henry V' with the London Symphony Orchestra in the Barbican. Tom Conti was to be the speaker in this performance. Lady Walton wanted to hold a reception following the concert inviting friends and people involved with the event.

As we had a great deal of work to do in the office we hired a temp for a few days. The temp arrived and was busy typing letters when Marjory was answering the telephone. Due to the reception we were having many calls accepting the invitation. Marjory was taking the calls and passing them over to me. We had a number of dignitaries attending so calls were coming through Lords and Ladies plus Buckingham Palace. Our temp seemed a little agitated and then went to the toilet, taking her bag with her. She had been gone quite some time so I asked Marjory to see if she was okay.

Marjory returned and said I'm afraid she's gone! I asked Marjory if she thought I was difficult to work with and did she think that is why she had departed? Marjory replied that I was not difficult to work for, but she thought that all the calls from important people had made her nervous. I said "Oh dear, you can't be fazed by anyone in this business". Marjory carried on typing until the phone rang again and she answered "It is Tom Conti for you!" "Just a minute Marjory let me compose myself" I replied.

After I had recovered I picked up the phone and spoke to Tom. He said "I am terribly sorry that I won't be able to attend the reception because I have eleven people coming to the concert". I then replied "Oh Tom, bring them all!" He was very grateful and thanked me profusely and said he looked forward to seeing me at the concert.

After I had put the phone down Marjory, still typing, retorted "who's not to be fazed by anyone in this business!" It certainly put me in my place!

Troilus and Cressida

At my surprise interview for the post of Artistic Director of the William Walton Trust one of my briefs was to get a performance of 'Troilus and Cressida' and make a success of it! We were very fortunate that Susana managed to get sponsorship for the Opera North Production with the Opera North Chorus and English Northern Philharmonia conducted by Richard Hickox. The soloists were Judith Howarth, Arthur Davies, Nigel Robson, Alan Opie and Yvonne Howard. All I had to do now was get two performances at Covent Garden and ensure that this production was a success – no pressure!

The score had to be revised for this Opera North Production. The première of 'Troilus and Cressida' was in 1954, with a libretto by Christopher Hassall based on Geoffrey Chaucer's 'Troilus and Cresyde'. Elisabeth Schwarzkopf was asked to sing in this production but her husband Walter Legge would not let her sing the role. It was therefore sung by the Hungarian soprano Magda Laszlo, and Richard Lewis was Troilus. Sir Malcolm Sargent conducted this performance at Covent Garden. During the rehearsals Sir Malcolm changed some of the scoring, but during the break Walton went round the music stands reverting the scores back again to the original. The musicians found the music very difficult to read as there were so many changed markings. This performance was not a critical success.

Later Dame Janet Baker asked Walton to change the soprano role to one for a mezzo for her to sing. Being a great admirer of Janet, Walton agreed to change the score but this meant not only changing the soprano line but also bridge passages and much more in the score. When this version was performed at Covent Garden, once again it was not a success.

Reverting back to a soprano version for the Opera North Production meant changing everything back again because, it appeared, the original score no longer existed. Christopher Palmer was given this huge task. He was one of the Walton Trustees at the time and I knew him and worked with him. Unfortunately in the middle of this mammoth job he died of AIDS. When he knew he would be unable to finish the work I had to go and collect all the music from him and get it to Stuart Hutchinson, who was to complete the work.

As PowerGen was our sponsor for educational projects I approached them for sponsorship of a Covent Garden performance and they agreed, and as HRH the Prince of Wales was a Patron of the William Walton Trust, he was delighted to accept his invitation to attend the Covent Garden performance. It was a busy time in the office and all hands were on deck as we had to organise a reception prior to the opera, in the interval and at the end. In addition there were presentations to HRH the Prince of Wales before the opera and in the interval.

I worked closely with the Private Secretary, Manon Williams, who happened to be the wife of Jeremy Huw Williams, who we were representing at the time. Manon was a tremendous help, and she also had a wicked sense of humour. On the big day I was waiting for HRH to arrive and Manon appeared. She looked at me and said "I have just dropped off the boss for a cup of tea with a friend, but don't worry he will be here soon".

I looked at her in horror because this was time for the first presentation. Seeing my look of horror she said "don't worry I'm only joking, he is just coming up the stairs now!" When I was presented to Prince Charles one of the questions he asked incredulously "What's it like working for her?" pointing to Lady Walton, who was in full flow talking to Sir Hugh Casson. Prince Charles knew what a forceful character she was, having been to Ischia and experienced Susana's forthright approach during his time there. My reply was one of genuine respect and admiration for her, even if she could be very trying at times!

A few days before this event we were working flat out in the office to get all the variations of invitations out to everyone. Marjory, my right-hand girl and someone I could not do without, and I worked until very late to make sure we had completed the task. All the invitations were duly posted the next day much to our relief. The following day I had a call from Buckingham Palace saying I had sent Lady Walton's tickets to HRH. Of course I nearly died in horror but the young girl at the end of the telephone was very sweet and said with humour in her voice "I don't think HRH will need a ticket, do you? But I shall post Lady Walton's back to you!" I was hoping this was the only slip up for this grand occasion!

Lady Walton was in her element sitting next to Prince Charles for an outstanding production because, after all, this had been written for her and she was thrilled to be telling everyone. Fortunately all the national music critics were at this performance and it received fantastic reviews. Phew! One of my tasks had been fulfilled.

Before moving on from 'Troilus and Cressida' I must mention one memorable performance I attended, which was in Nottingham, one of the venues for the production's tour. The first act of the opera was nearing its end when I realised that Cressida, Judith Howarth, was losing her voice. The curtain came down at the end of Act I and the interval was going on for some time, so I went backstage to see what was happening.

I was told by Ian Killick, manager of the orchestra, that Judith would not be able to sing in the second act so Yvonne Howard, the wonderful mezzo who was playing Evadne, was to sing the role from a box at the side of the stage and Judith would act the role on stage.

The only problem was that they could not find the cover for Evadne! Eventually she was tracked down in a Chinese restaurant up the road! After an interval of approximately 45 minutes the performance commenced with Yvonne singing from a box at the side of the stage. She saved the day and sang the role magnificently.

Oldham Festival

Another major development of the Trust was the start of the Oldham Festival. This was initiated by Paul Barnet from the Oldham Council and Ian Killick; both were great fans of William Walton. As he was born in Oldham on 29 March 1902 at Werneth Road Oldham, it was the obvious place to hold a Walton Festival. Without support from the Trust this might not have taken place but Susana and I attended every event each year and it was a great success. Lord Harewood became the Patron and he also attended each year as did Michael Kennedy, Humphrey Burton and other celebrated people in the music world.

The main orchestra performing each year was the English Northern Philharmonia, the orchestra of Opera North, and of course many of Walton's works were performed during the festivals. One year we had the Coronation March 'Orb and Sceptre' included with the showing of the Coronation of Queen Elizabeth. I remember sitting next to Lord Harewood and, as the Queen was walking the length of Westminster Abbey with page boys holding her train, George turned to me and whispered "I am that page boy on the right just behind Her Majesty".

Susana and I had many exciting and humorous experiences in Oldham. One experience was when we were in Paul Barnet's car being taken back to Oldham after attending a recording session with Black Dyke Mills Band of Walton music. Susana said "I feel very hungry after all that session". Paul replied "would you like fish and chips?" Bearing in mind Susana was Argentinian, she said "that sounds good, I've never had fish and chips".

Paul pulled the car up in a layby, where there happened to be a fish and chip shop close by. He ran into the shop and came back a few minutes later with three packets of fish and chips wrapped in newspaper and dumped them on our laps. "What do we do with this?" enquired Susana. "You open them up and eat the fish and chips with your fingers!" was the answer. Susana thought they were delicious and had discovered a new Northern experience.

Another experience was eating pie, mash and mushy peas with Susana and George in a very large, packed village hall, while listening to Black Dyke Mills

Band performing in an Oldham Festival concert. The concerts in the festival needless to say were brilliant with many international ensembles and artists but also local northern talent taking part. However, one of the most amazing times was when Susana and I had a curried tea!

The house in Werneth Road where Walton was born had a blue plaque above the door and the proud owner at this time was an Indian family. The family sent a message to say that they would be honoured to have Lady Walton and myself to afternoon tea, when we were in Oldham for the Festival. We gratefully accepted and a time was arranged.

The day arrived and we turned up at 3.30pm as planned. Mr Rhab, (I shall use this name) was at the door to greet us with a huge bouquet for Lady Walton. As we entered the house there was a wonderful smell of curry wafting through the building and Susana whispered to me "I hope we are not having curry because we have just had lunch". We were taken into the front room with a large coffee table in the centre. We were asked to sit down, and then Mrs Rhab was introduced to Lady Walton. This was followed by Mr Rhab's children and then his mother, but then the neighbours were invited in one by one to greet Lady Walton, all with hands clasped bowing as they were introduced. This went on for nearly half an hour.

After all the introductions Mrs Rhab arrived with bottles of 'pop' and then the children bringing many different kinds of beautiful curries. Susana whispered she couldn't eat curry now but I whispered back that we had to eat something because, if not, we would appear very rude. We struggled with the dishes, but after a while Susana announced "I thought we were coming for tea?" At this Mr Rhab rushed out and returned five minutes later with a pot of tea, two cups and saucers and a plate of biscuits. Soon after this we decided it was time to take our leave, so we congratulated him on his curries and thanked him for the tea and biscuits and departed. The memory of our curried afternoon tea is a memory I shall never forget.

The Centenary Year

There are so many wonderful memories and stories about my time with Lady Walton and the Walton Trust but they would fill a whole book to themselves. One of the other things we organised was the wonderful photograph exhibition being held by Sotheby's. This included photographs of Walton, Whistler, Cecil Beaton, Osbert, Sacheverell and Edith Sitwell plus other arty people of that period. We had mounted an exhibition in the National Portrait Gallery combined with a performance of 'Facade' with English Serenata conducted by Guy Woolfenden and Susana Walton and Richard Baker as the speakers.

During Walton's centenary year in 2002 the exhibition was in the foyer of the Royal Festival Hall to complement the first concert of the celebration concerts. This was with the London Symphony Orchestra conducted by André Previn when Walton's Violin, Viola and Cello concertos were all performed in the same concert.

The photograph exhibition moved around various festivals and concerts throughout the centenary year and at the end of 2002 it went to Christ Church, Oxford, in the Walton Room. Walton had been chorister and undergraduate at Christ Church for many years and was known to say that Oxford was the best place in all the world.

In 2002 I was fortunate enough to be responsible for many Walton concerts throughout the UK and further afield. These included a performances of 'Facade', with Lady Walton in the Sydney Opera House and the Concertgebouw, Amsterdam. Among other concerts was one in Germany with the Deutsches Rundfunk Orchester conducted by Sakari Oramo with Stephen Isserlis, performing the 'Walton Cello Concerto'. Another was in Denmark with the Aarhus Symphony Orchestra conducted by James Loughran with Maxim Vengerov performing both the Mendelssohn Violin and Walton Viola Concertos. This was a particularly spectacular concert which I attended with Susana. By this time Gwyn had retired from the CBSO and was able to join us. This was particularly good for him because he was meeting up again with Jimmy Loughran who had been in Bournemouth, as an associate conductor to Silvestri, when Gwyn was in the BSO.

It was spectacular because Vengerov performed the Mendelssohn Violin Concerto in the first half, the Walton Viola Concerto in the second half, followed by an unaccompanied Bach encore on a baroque violin. This was quite an amazing feat for anyone. After the concert there was a reception and I was sitting with Vengerov so I asked him what it was like playing on different string instruments in the same concert. He said when he played the violin it was like driving a sports car, when he played the viola in was like driving a great big truck. I took it that he was far more comfortable with the violin, although he did make a wonderful sound on the viola.

Lady Walton and I were present, sometimes separately and sometimes together, at many Walton concerts that year. We started the year in January with the LSO concert and we finished the Walton Centenary Year at Harewood House, the home of Lord and Lady Harewood, with a performance of 'Facade' with Lady Walton and the baritone Jeremy Huw Williams as speakers, with the English Northern Philharmonia Orchestra conducted by David Lloyd Jones. I knew Susana was not comfortable at this concert, which was most unusual, but it was the start of her osteoporosis and she was finding it difficult to stand for each number. In addition her fascinator was slipping down onto her forehead.

After the performance, as always, I helped her with her dress. She wore Mariano Fortuny pleated silk dresses for her performances; to pack them away, they had be tied into a knot and put into a bag. On this occasion they were damp because she had been perspiring so we had to dry the dress before putting it away.

The night prior to the concert we were in Harewood House but, after the concert Susana wanted me to get to Stansted airport ready for her flight back to Naples and then on to Ischia. On the long drive from Yorkshire to Stansted we chatted and she asked me if she was still any good at performing 'Facade'. I replied "You are as good as ever but you must remain seated when you perform because you are finding it now too difficult to stand for each number". She then said, much to my surprise "if that's the case I shall never perform 'Facade' again" and she never did.

I had been thinking at this time that the Centenary Year would be a good time to end my twelve years with the William Walton Trust. As Susana would no longer need me to accompany her for 'Facade' performances it seemed even more reason to end my very enjoyable but pressurised work with the Trust. In addition I was being asked to raise funds for the La Mortella gardens in Ischia. This is not what I had been taken on to do and I decided it was time to move on. Dear Susana would not accept my resignation for a few months but eventually knew that my mind was made up.

I was very pleased that Susana and I remained close and I often met her at the Savoy, whenever she came to England. Her visits became less and less frequent, as her health deteriorated. I was of course very sad when she passed away on 21st March 2010. My work with Susana and the Trust was very demanding but very rewarding and introduced me to many new and unforgettable experiences.

Chapter 16

RICHARD BAKER OBE, RD

After thirty years both Richard and Margaret were a very large part of the lives of both Gwyn and myself, and indeed all the family.

Our lives seem to have run parallel, because we were married the same year, and our daughter Julia and their son James were both born in the early summer of 1964. Our grandchildren all seemed to arrive at the same time and Margaret and I often compared notes on the families. If Richard was performing in the Warwickshire area Margaret and Richard frequently stayed at our home in Wilmcote. At Christmas our present to them would be a couple of days in Wilmcote with a visit to the Royal Shakespeare Theatre. Richard and Margaret loved joining Gwyn and myself at the RST because Richard himself was quite an actor and loved nothing more than seeing a Shakespeare play performed really well.

As Richard was such an amazing man, broadcaster, radio and TV personality, author, fine musician and a unique personality it is right that a chapter should be devoted to him. He wrote a number of books, mainly on music but he never wrote his autobiography so, with the help of his family, I shall try to build a picture of this special man with a devoted wife who supported him throughout his life. They say behind every great man there is a 'great woman' and Margaret was certainly no exception.

I know a great deal about Richard's music career but I have enlisted the help of his son Andrew to fill me in with his fascinating days at sea. The P&O Music Festivals at Sea brought together Richard's love of both music and the sea and he was in his element with both. The cruises came just a few years after I started representation of Richard so I asked Andrew, an editor at the *Telegraph*, to write a piece for me about this extraordinary man's life at sea and here it is word for word with Andrew's permission.

My father's broadcasting career is fairly well-known – this is the sea-going story...

Richard's love of the sea began in childhood, when he was fascinated by the pleasure steamers that sailed from the River Thames to ports around the south coast of England. He dreamed that one day he might captain such a vessel.

Instead he won a scholarship from Kilburn Grammar School to read History at Peterhouse, Cambridge. After just two terms, at 18 he was called up. After basic training at HM Ganges (shore establishment) he was posted to a minesweeper and had the rank of midshipman. He then joined HMS Peacock in Tobermory, Scotland, to train other sloops in readiness for supporting convoys to Russia. Richard was only 19 at this time.

Training in Tobermory was an eventful experience.

On one occasion, as midshipman (the most junior of officers) he was covered in bright purple iodine wound dressing as a prank – and then unexpectedly summoned by the admiral in charge of the training base, a fearsome character known as The Terror of Tobermory, whose biography Richard would later write.

"Well now," said the admiral, scrutinising the quaking purple figure before him. "Tell me, what are your duties aboard ship?"

"I'm gunnery officer," Richard reported. "And ... Entertainments Officer."

"Humph," the admiral snorted. "I can see you take one part of your job seriously."

On the sloop HMS Peacock Richard sailed on Atlantic convoy protection duty on the harsh Arctic route to Murmansk.

In the course of three years' service he was promoted to lieutenant and, as gunnery officer, played a part in the sinking of two U-boats and was awarded the Atlantic star. He never talked of that side of his service, preferring to recount tales of comrade's fondness for practising the French horn in a cramped mess-room.

Years later, he and the few surviving colleagues of those duties were belatedly awarded the Arctic Star by the government, and the Ushakov Medal of the Russian Navy. Richard liked to joke that the latter was given to him mainly in recognition of his managing to read Tolstoy's War and Peace en route to Murmansk.

Returning eventually to his studies and then commencing his broadcasting career. Richard remained in the Royal Navy Reserve and was often called up for brief episodes of service. He was promoted once again to lieutenant-commander, RNR, and enjoyed many adventures in this role, including a spell on the cruiser Tiger, and once catapulting in a jet from the deck of the carrier Ark Royal.

Most hazardously of all, perhaps, he boarded a nuclear submarine while it was underway on the surface, lowered towards the conning tower from a helicopter hovering above.

"*Permission to come aboard, sir?*" *he yelled to the commanding officer, while dangling above the bridge.*

"*I suppose you'd better, now you've come all this way,*" *the officer replied.*

Richard wrote two naval biographies: the bestselling The Terror of Tobermory (1972), a humorous wartime account of Vice Admiral Sir Gilbert 'Puggy' Stephenson, under whom he had served when working-up Peacock; and Dry Ginger (1977), an affectionate and perceptive account of his friend 'Lef'. Admiral of the Fleet Sir Michael Le Fanu, one of the most brilliant and unorthodox naval officers of his generation.

He kept naval hours throughout his life, rising extraordinarily early even in his 90s to write letters or tinker with a memoir. He was often puzzled when family members were reluctant to join him for a cup of tea at 6am.

On his eventual retirement from the RNR Richard was awarded the coveted Reserve Decoration, and for years subsequently he would proudly don his uniform once a year to take the salute at the local Remembrance Day parade. He was proud of his clinker-built sailing boat, Little Rose, and throughout his life the sight of the sea would bring a dreamy expression to his eyes; he relished his frequent invitations to join officers on the bridge of the P&O cruise ships on which he was embarked.

I shall now continue with the other aspects of Richard's career, but mainly musical. Apart from being the first newsreader on BBC Television (he would go on to read the news for 25 years), he was a panellist on the much-loved quiz Face the Music, presented many popular programmes such as Start the Week on radio, introduced the Last Night of the Proms and also regularly presented the New Years Day Concert from Vienna, plus the Remembrance Day concert from the Royal Albert Hall each year. In addition he presented concerts and could narrate most of the orchestral and chamber music narrator works. He also seemed to find time to give duo performances with the pianist Raphael Terroni and the singer/guitarist Caroline McCausland and other instrumentalists, as well as giving charity concerts for many organisations, with which he was involved.

Richard wrote a number of books, some mentioned above, but also on Schubert, Mozart, The Magic of Music, Richard Baker's Companion to Music and a Music quiz book, initiated by the syndicate music quizzes on the Music Festivals at Sea. He even wrote a book on London – A Theme and Variations.

I think Margaret would agree with me that he was a workaholic but he enjoyed all aspects of his work apart from, he once told me, giving out for the first time dreadful news when reading on the BBC. He told me how he had been very badly affected having to read out about the school in Aberfan that was buried by a coal landslide in 1966, with most of the children and staff killed.

With Richard's work I was kept very busy but a lot of the work seemed to be interlocking, which made life easier. Richard performed on the cruises and also with Lady Walton in 'Facade' plus other organisations with which I was already working.

Shortly after I began looking after Richard's engagements he took on an evening performance in the Town Hall, Birmingham, with the City of Birmingham Symphony Orchestra. Gwyn was naturally playing in this concert and it was a performance of the choral and narrator work, Honegger's 'King David'. It was with the City of Birmingham Choir conducted by Christopher Robinson. Richard narrated the whole work, plus performing the part of the Witch of Endor, totally from memory. This was quite an amazing thing to do and showed how talented he was.

Another time I remember was when he was presenting Start the Week on radio. On a Saturday he was provided with all the recent books written by the authors, who were going to be interviewed by him on the Monday morning programme. It was quite a large and wide ranging array of books and it was Richard's job to read the books over the weekend and be ready to ask intelligent questions on the Monday morning, which he always did. I asked him one day how on earth was he able to take in so much and remember it all for the programme. "Oh it's easy" he said "I spend the weekend cramming it all in my head for a Monday morning but, if you ask me about any of the books on the Tuesday, I won't remember anything". Whether that was true or not I don't know but, what I do know, is that he was a very clever man.

In spite of all this talent he had a great sense of humour and this was shown in one of the Morecambe and Wise television Christmas programmes, when he performed in 'There is Nothing like a Dame'. He could also tell humorous stories onstage with perfect timing. One of the stories he told against himself was about a post office in Wales. He was on holiday with the family and he went into a post office for some cards and stamps. The young lady postmistress asked, with a thick Welsh accent, "Aren't you Richard Baker?" Looking rather embarrassed he replied "Hum, well yes I am"; the girl's very quick reply was "WHAT a disappointment!"

Passengers on the Music Festivals at Sea and audiences at his duo concerts were often treated to some of his very amusing readings such as 'Disaster at Sea' and the Dorset countryman's impression on his first hearing of Handel's 'Messiah'. As he got older he found stories about old age. Richard was the consummate performer and was much in demand for his unique talent.

There were even times with very bad weather when Richard would still reach his venue. There was the time when the winds brought down trees all over the country. On that occasion Richard had an engagement in Swindon so he set out with Margaret early in the morning. On their way they found the road blocked by trees and had to seek another route and the same thing kept happening so they re-routed many times. It took all day to get from London to Swindon but they eventually arrived, much to their relief. What did they find on arrival? The Manager of the hall outside shaking his head and saying "no performance tonight because the roof has come off the building".

There are many more tales to tell but I think between Andrew and myself you will have formed a picture of this unique performer, whom I was so honoured to represent for over 30 years.

Chapter 17

THE FAMILY

In the nineties we had three family weddings and three births, the third wedding after the girls' being my brother Dennis marrying Diane. Dennis married Diane in 1992, when he was in his forties. We never thought he would ever marry but, when he found the right girl, that was it. Both Dennis and Diane have been a great support to me in all ways but Diane, in particular, over the past ten years or so has helped me greatly with administration. Both Dennis and Diane were high level civil servants. Diane was secretary to the Foreign Minister so I could not have had anyone better to oversee my business affairs.

The birth of Daniel William in 1993, mentioned before, was when Gwyn and I were in Brighton at a 'Facade' performance. Dan's sister Lucy Claire was born in October 1997 and this time neither of us were travelling so we were able to get to see her soon after the birth. The birth was not particularly easy as Julia had pneumonia and was still quite poorly when she gave birth. However all was well as far as Lucy was concerned and Julia slowly recovered from pneumonia.

When Rachel visited the hospital to see Julia I could see the maternal look in her eyes when holding Lucy. We didn't realise at that time that she was pregnant with Henry George, who was born in June 1998. We now had three lovely grandchildren to keep us busy in addition to all the music activities. As Dan and Lucy lived nearby we saw a great deal of them both and we were frequently required to baby sit.

When Dan was small he loved sitting at the piano with me and playing little tunes, 'Three Blind Mice' being a favourite. He also loved to sing and 'Kumbaya' was a song he loved. A few years later, when still only six he won a children's talent contest singing 'Kumbaya'. Dan had a lovely voice and, when he was a little older he sang 'Silent Worship' by Handel. At one stage we did consider a choir school for Dan but Julia wanted her children at home so it was out of the question. Dan was learning piano with me and violin with Gwyn and he enjoyed trio sessions with us when I played piano, Dan violin and Gwyn the viola. He remembers these sessions fondly to this day.

Eldest grandson Dan is now a mechanical engineer. Last year he passed his apprenticeship with flying colours, achieving 90% and scored the highest marks for five years so I am very proud of him, as I am of all the grandchildren.

Lucy was not as outgoing as Dan, as a baby, and she was late in talking. However she would look at us with disdain when we asked her to say certain words. When she was about eighteen months she came out with sentences and from then on never stopped talking. She had been taking it all in and then decided to use all the words she had heard. Both Dan and Lucy loved making marzipan sweets with me. There was one occasion when Dan was sitting up to the breakfast bar making sweets and Gwyn was videoing. I was at the sink and asking Dan if he was okay. "Yes fine Nanny" was his reply. What I did not see was Dan making the sweets and dipping them into the caster sugar and then licking the sugar off both hands before dipping the next sweet in the sugar. I was horrified when I saw the video but Gwyn seemed quite unconcerned about the health and safety aspect!

Dan was only five when it was discovered by accident that he had a hole in the heart. He had been taken to the Doctor for a small complaint but he wanted to try the stethoscope on his chest. The Doctor then discovered an irregular heart beat and said it needed investigating. Soon after he was admitted to the Birmingham Children's Hospital for very serious open heart surgery.

Jimmy's Mum was looking after Lucy while Gwyn and I were at the hospital with Jimmy and Julia for several hours through the life and death operation. This was a terribly tense and worrying time and we were all very relieved when we heard that the operation was over and it was a success. Two days later Dan was up and about and, when asked if he would like to be the magician's assistant, he jumped at the opportunity. The operation scar right down his chest he always called his zip!

Lucy started to play the piano when she was older than Dan had been but she took to it like a duck to water. Like Dan she had a very good ear for music but her hands were strong and always positioned correctly. She made great progress and even came to church on a Sunday to play duets on the organ with me at the end of the service. However, when she was about ten, she decided that she didn't want to play anymore. This was a big disappointment to Gwyn and myself at the time as she was so talented but the lessons were all worthwhile. Lucy is now a very good paediatric nurse but whenever she comes to the house she goes straight to the piano to play. She plays duets with me and gets a great deal of enjoyment out of her music.

I should mention that Lucy also had a very good voice and, when she was about eleven, she joined the English Serenata Youth Choir. This introduced her to a great deal of choral music but she also had the opportunity of singing in the Buxton Opera House with the choir. All the family attended the performance and we all felt very proud.

Rachel lived in Reading, where her husband was a teacher, so we didn't see as much of Henry as we did Dan and Lucy, although he did occasionally come to stay. He was not an easy child but we discovered later that this had a lot to do with his intelligence and frustration. When he went to school he was always in trouble and would not sit still to listen to the fairy story at the end of the afternoon. One day I asked him "Henry why don't you listen to the fairy story?" His reply "I don't like fairy stories because they are not real". "What books do you like Henry?" I asked. Without hesitation he came back with "I like dictionaries and encyclopaedias!"

Another instance when he was at primary school was again during a fairy story. At the end of day, he got under the table and tied all the children's shoe laces together and when they stood up they were all tied together. Once again he was in trouble.

When Henry went to secondary school he was able to understand his frustrations and able to direct his intelligence in the right way. His football was a great boon to him because he was obsessed with it and became exceptionally good at the game. He wanted nothing more than to play football with his brother, which then enthused Harvey. The football was later dropped when he had other interests. He got a place at Huddersfield University to take a masters in Pharmaceutical research and moving on to do a doctorate.

In 1999 we had three lovely grandchildren with Rachel expecting her second in June. Gwyn and I decided we had to do something special with all the family for the Millennium. We discussed this and, as Gwyn and I loved Madeira, we thought this would be a wonderful place to go for beautiful weather and fireworks. Looking into the costs we found the flights alone for the nine of us were going to be over £8,000 and that was without accommodation. We decided this was too much so we looked at other possibilities.

We came to the conclusion that, as Copenhagen was our favourite city, why not look into that. Flights for the nine us going from Stansted airport came to £700 and then we looked at accommodation. We found two citalets in the centre of Copenhagen at a reasonable cost so this is what we all decided would be ideal, even though it would be a cold millennium, as opposed to a fine weather one in Madeira.

Soon after the trip was organised Dan was asked by a family friend "What are you doing for the millennium?" His reply "we were going to Madeira, where it is very warm but we are now going to Copenhagen and freeze to death!"

We had a wonderful time with our three grandchildren aged 7 and 3 and 2 with Harvey on the way. Copenhagen was a wonderful city to celebrate the turn of the century and we were able to meet up with our Danish friends. We saw the changing of the guard at the Amalienborg Palace, skated on the ice rink opposite the five star D'Angleterre hotel, which was decorated with Hans Christian Andersen's 'Snow Maiden', went to the spectacular Copenhagen Zoo and of course visited the Tivoli Gardens, with all the Christmas markets. The firework display was magnificent and went on well into the early hours. I baby sat with the two little ones while the others took Dan out for an experience of a lifetime. Fortunately the citalet was on the second floor and overlooking Tivoli Gardens so, when the babies were sleeping, I had a ringside view of the fireworks.

What a wonderful way to celebrate the Millennium.

Our first grandchild of the new century was born in May 2000. This was Harvey Joseph and was a little brother for Henry. Our family was now growing and was giving us great joy. Gwyn loved nothing more than videoing the children at every opportunity. On one occasion Gwyn was baby sitting with Harvey and got out his camera. Harvey decided to climb up the stair rail but, only three at the time, this was dangerous. Instead of gently telling him to come down Gwyn decided to video him, and at the same time, have a conversation about jam tarts! Gwyn asked him if he made jam tarts and Harvey gave a him a long description of jam tart making but, at the same time climbing higher up the stairs. We were all amused but horrified watching this video. Gwyn saw nothing wrong! Once again health and safety didn't come into it.

Before the birth of our fifth grandchild we had a death in the family. Our daughter Kathryn, now nearly thirty was living at Four Gables, housing five residents with learning difficulties. This was very well staffed and they were all very caring so we were happy with this home we had found in Snitterfield, just five minutes from our house in Wilmcote. We visited regularly and at weekends took her out for drives in the car, which she very much enjoyed. At Four Gables Kathryn reached her full potential and we feel there could not be anywhere better for her.

It was on the 13 February in 2001 when I was in my office in Stratford that I had a call from Four Gables. We knew Kathryn was suffering from a cold but I was not expecting the call that afternoon to tell me Kathryn had passed away, because she had developed pneumonia and could not fight the infection. At the time I was having a meeting with Pam Staff from PowerGen, our Walton sponsor, and I was stunned. Pam immediately said I am taking you home now and we can wait for Gwyn to come home from rehearsal, which would be at about 5pm and then I can take you both to Four Gables. When we arrived home Gwyn was already there so Pam stayed in the car and I went in to tell Gwyn this startling news and, like me, he was stunned.

We called the girls and, Julia who lived nearby, wanted to come with us to Four Gables. It was lovely that Kathryn passed away in her own room, in her own bed and with all her favourite things around her. She also had the love of all the brilliant staff so we had the consolation that her final years were very happy years in her own little world.

A year later we put on a wonderful concert in the Adrian Boult Hall, Birmingham, to raise funds for a sensory garden at Four Gables. Many of our brilliant musical friends wanted to be involved and Richard Baker presented the evening. We had an orchestra made up of members of the CBSO led by Peter Thomas and conducted by Guy Woolfenden. Ingrid Surgenor was the pianist and RST's Andy Stone-Fewings played trumpet, when Jaqueline Fugelle sang Mozart's 'Allelujah'. Mark Evans and Wynne Evans (of Go-Compare fame) gave a moving performance of the 'Pearl Fishers Duet'.

Ted Watson, clarinet with the RSC wrote a beautiful piece called 'For Kathryn'. This was for harp, clarinet and mezzo. Robert Johnston, CBSO harpist, Ted Watson clarinet and Kate Flowers mezzo performed this work. In addition we had a young string quartet from the junior department of the Birmingham Conservatoire performing 'Country Gardens'. My great friend Mary had a granddaughter, Lizzy who was a very talented little viola player and she had formed the quartet.

As the concert was for a garden we wanted the programme to be all about flowers, water and gardens. It was a lovely programme including Peter Thomas performing 'The Lark Ascending' and ending with all performers, plus the young quartet, joining the professionals in Bernstein's 'Make our Garden Grow' from Candide. It was an amazing evening and we raised over £5,000 for the garden. The only disappointment was that the evening was not recorded.

The sensory garden was designed by Diane Long, head of sponsorship for PowerGen, who later started up her own business as a landscape garden designer. The garden was officially opened by Richard Baker and international guitarist, Craig Ogden, played music in the garden. It has trellises with hanging baskets and lights and a wrought iron gate with KAW, Kathryn Anne Williams, is a feature of the gardens. It also has a water feature and many herbs because the garden was especially designed for the residents so that, especially those with impaired vision, are able to feel and smell the plants and special features.

In July 2002 our second granddaughter was born and a sister for Henry and Harvey. This time we were on a Music Festival at Sea! We were at the top of Norway on this occasion and late that evening Rachel's husband called to say you have another granddaughter. I said "wonderful, what is she called?" He said "Skye". I replied "could you spell that please?" He then spelt out SKYE saying it was like the Isle of Skye and not like the sky above! She was actually called Skye Kathryn, named after her auntie who had died the year before.

Now having five grandchildren we thought that would be all but another two were to follow. In November 2006 Daisy Mae was born. As usual we were at sea so the news reached us in the middle of a concert. Many of the passengers were anxious to hear the news so Richard made an announcement on stage about the birth of Daisy Mae. Our passenger friends on the ship were very kind and some sent cards and one lovely Welsh lady, Nina, knitted baby clothes for Daisy.

Daisy loves dancing and spends a lot of time singing and dancing to music so who knows what she will do later! She is very girlie, loves pretty clothes and loves arts and crafts. Birthday and Christmas cards from Daisy are beautifully made by hand.

All Rachel's children apart from Daisy are very sporty, which is not surprising with Rachel being a Personal Fitness Trainer. The three boys have been very much into football and Harvey even got into Oxford United Football Academy and was there for five years. Charlie is now an aspiring young football player.

Skye is really good at netball and plays for a club in addition to the school team. She too is very arty but also meticulous and keeps her bedroom immaculate. She has done some very good work for her A levels and has gained offers to both Bournemouth and Portsmouth Universities plus another three, and has decided upon Bournemouth. It looks as if sport will be her chosen career.

Was Daisy the last? No – in March 2010 Charles Ethan was born. For this birth I was very much involved as I was needed to look after the other four children so I went to stay a few days before the birth. As predicted, with babies, labour pains started late evening so Rachel was rushed off to the Radcliffe hospital. She produced Charlie in the early hours of the morning and was on her way home with baby a few hours later, much to the excitement of the other children.

Charlie is a gorgeous red head with a fiery but lovely nature to match. He is now a typical little boy and full of mischief. He is very clever with a screwdriver and had to be watched when he was small because he would unscrew everything in sight! Charlie has a friend called Rudy and, when they are together, they get up to all sorts of things.

I was at the house one day and the two boys were playing upstairs, when I heard a bang from above. I didn't think anything about it at the time but I then went upstairs to the bathroom and to my horror saw a hole and crack in the bathroom window. When Rachel saw this she called the two boys up to the bathroom. "Who did this?" she asked. Apologetically Charlie replied "I did but Rudy did it first. He threw a marble at the window but it didn't break but then I had a go and it went through the window". Having given Charlie some pocket money earlier I said "you know what you must do now Charlie and that is to give Mummy your money to help pay for the window". Without hesitation he ran to get his money and handed it over to his Mum and said how sorry he was. He may be mischievous but he is a very loveable child and adored by his siblings.

Having spent so much time at sea it is inevitable that I sometimes took the family on a holiday cruise to see Nanny's ships! All of the children experienced the sea from an early age and having visited so many different countries it must have given them a great deal of geographical knowledge. In later years the older children i.e. Dan, Lucy and Henry have come on my cruises and worked with me. I have found these three have all done a grand job and loved the interaction with the artists. They have learnt a great deal about concert management and how artists tick and are very interested in this work.

On one cruise Dan was the Roadie for Maraca2, a percussion duo with Tim Palmer and Jason Huxtable. They were giving a demonstration concert one night, which involved passenger participation. They decided to use Ravel's 'Bolero' for the main piece in the programme and Dan was taught the important snare drum part that runs throughout the piece. He was only sixteen at the time and he played the part brilliantly. The whole team turned out to hear this performance and it was a great thrill for Dan when he was cheered wholeheartedly by the artists and passengers.

I hope my work has given my daughters and the grandchildren a wider experience of life and equipped them with an artistic knowledge to take forward into the future.

Chapter 18

SOUNDS OF SWEDEN

The other major event for us in the 1990s was the Swedish Festival in April 1997. I had worked in Scandinavia for a few years, and largely in Sweden with the Swedish Concert Institute called Svenska Rikskonserter. I was approached by Martin Martinsson, Director of Rikskonserter, early in 1996, who asked if a Swedish festival could be arranged in England. With the relatively new Birmingham Symphony Hall, and the contacts I had in the Midlands I suggested we strongly considered Birmingham for such a grand event.

Martin and I had a meeting at Symphony Hall with its director, Andrew Jowett. He was very enthusiastic and the date for the festival was fixed for 5-19 April 1997, and we decided it would be called Sounds of Sweden. A senior member of Rikskonserter, Hugo Ramsten and I were appointed joint Artistic Directors of this unique venture. Just over a year to plan an event as large as this was going to take a great deal of work to bring if off successfully.

I worked very closely with Anders Classon, Cultural Attaché at the Swedish Embassy and with Andrew Jowett at Symphony Hall. A number of meetings were organised in Stockholm at Rikskonserter with Martin Martinsson and Hugo Ramsten, at the Swedish Embassy and at Symphony Hall with Andrew Jowett and Lyndon Jenkins, artistic advisor there. Early on in the discussions we managed to get HRH Princess Christina of Sweden as Patron, Elisabeth Söderström CBE as President, His Excellency, Mr Mats Bergqvist, Ambassador of Sweden and Mrs Marion Arnott-Job, Lord Mayor of Birmingham as our Vice-Presidents.

The Royal Gala Opening was planned in Symphony Hall with the BBC Concert Orchestra conducted by Barry Wordsworth with Elisabeth Söderström and Ulrika Jonsson as joint presenters. The orchestra gave an evening of Swedish music with the legendary Swedish tenor Nicolai Gedda, soprano Ulla Westland

and The Real Group, a vocal quintet of singers from Sweden, and the City of Birmingham Choir. This programme was to set the Swedish Festival on its way with a broadcast by BBC Radio 2.

Other events were the Voice of Sweden with the Ex Cathedral Soloists, Choir & Baroque Orchestra, Sandvik Children's Choir and Birmingham Schools Chorale conducted by Jeffrey Skidmore. Orchestras involved were the City of Birmingham Symphony Orchestra (Gwyn playing), conducted by Paavo Jarvi; Birmingham Contemporary Music Group; the Swedish Radio Symphony Orchestra conducted by Okko Kamu, with Katarina Karneus, a former winner of Cardiff Singer of the World.

A number of venues in Birmingham were used for the events in addition to Symphony Hall: the Barber Institute of Fine Arts with 'Swedish Masters' performed by the Birmingham Ensemble and Peter Thomas violin; the Cathedral of St Philip for the Organ Recital with Gunnar Idenstam; the Adrian Boult Hall for Birmingham Contemporary Music Group conducted by Elgar Howarth with Christian Lindberg and Håkan Hardenberger; the Yggdrasil Swedish String Quartet and the Internationally renowned Swedish Percussion Ensemble Kroumata; Birmingham Conservatoire with many Swedish events mainly with Swedish students.

A wide range of Swedish composers featured in the programmes such as Franz Berwald, Karin Rehnqvist, Ian Sandström, Wilhelm Stenhammar and many others. In addition there was a world première by the Greek composer Iannis Xenakis, which BBC Radio 3 broadcast. This was performed by Christian Lindberg, one of the world's greatest trombonists. There were a number of other world premières including one by Folke Rabe and Ian Sandström.

The idea of Sounds of Sweden coming to Birmingham was for a unique two-week festival of music to celebrate the cultural and historic links between Britain and Sweden. Birmingham, through its world-class venue, was proud to play host for Britain. The city welcomed an array of internationally renowned orchestras and soloists, who brought Swedish music in a blend of the familiar, the popular and the innovative.

As the festival was approaching, Andrew Jowett and I met to discuss a press launch. He said we could use the smaller hall for the press conference late morning. Anders Classon from the Embassy agreed to lay on the food and drink following the launch. Andrew suggested that I try to get sponsorship from British Rail for a first class carriage to transport London press to and from Birmingham in time for the press to get back to London, in order to attend any evening concerts they may be reviewing.

I worked on this idea and managed to obtain BR sponsorship. I then went to Volvo in Warwick to ask for a coach to take the press from New Street station to Symphony Hall and return there after the press conference. Fortunately, at that time the Managing Director of Volvo, Bernt Brandsieg was a friend who lived in Wilmcote, so I had a head start. Having now organised the train and the coach we were in a position to send out invitations to the media.

Andrew's next idea was that he should go to London early morning, on the day of the press launch, with Martin Denny, my young assistant, who was indispensable (and is now Artistic Director of the Windsor Festival). Andrew would take champagne to London and Martin would buy fresh orange juice at Euston Station. They would meet the media at an appointed time and place at Euston Station, and on the journey from London to Birmingham, Andrew and Martin would hand out Buck's Fizz with the help of BR, providing the glasses.

I was at Symphony Hall waiting to greet the local media and await the arrival of the London contingent. When they arrived at the Hall everyone was very merry and greeted me like a long lost friend. The press conference was a great success and was followed by an excellent lunch. Timings worked perfectly and the London contingent returned in plenty of time to review their evening performances. Consequently we had excellent media coverage for Sounds of Sweden. The council also did us proud by displaying 100 large Sounds of Sweden posters with illuminated signs throughout the city.

HRH Princess Christina, attended the Gala Opening Concert and I had the honour of hosting her for the few days she was in Birmingham. She was a great lover of William Morris. Morris had visited his friend Thomas Wardle at his home in Leek, Staffordshire and a collaboration began with the two men. The house is full of arts and crafts. I arranged a visit to the Thomas Wardle home in Leek for Princess Christina, as this house was of great interest to her and she was able see much of William Morris's work.

The visit was planned for the day after the Gala Opening Concert, which was much enjoyed by the Princess. A light lunch was arranged for our party, which included Princess Christina, the Swedish Ambassador and a number of embassy officials. I nearly blotted my copy book when, thinking it was time to depart, I stood up to gather everyone together. I was quickly told by the cultural attaché to sit down because I must wait for the Princess to stand first! At that point the Princess rose and was ready to depart. We were taken in chauffeur-driven limos with the Swedish flag on the front of the car taking the Princess and the Ambassador.

I was in the first car with embassy officials because I was meant to lead the way – with the Royal car following – no satnav at that time! All was going well until we came to a roundabout and I was not sure which exit to take so we went round a couple of times before I decided which exit to take. Unfortunately the car behind had to follow. I thought to myself it was the second time that day I had blotted my copy book!

The house had been opened especially for us as it was a Sunday. When we arrived there we were greeted very graciously by the curator and his wife and given a very extensive tour, followed by afternoon tea. Princess Christina was delighted with the visit having seen some of the best examples of William Morris silks, cottons, curtains and other examples of his work.

The Festival was a great success and achieved the aim of raising the profile of Swedish culture in the United Kingdom. The following November I was called from the Embassy to say that I was to be awarded a decoration from the King of Sweden. This was the Order of the Polar or North Star, as it is sometimes called. A reception was arranged at the home of the Ambassador and I could invite whoever I wanted to the presentation, which was a splendid affair. I felt very honoured to receive this decoration, especially as the last lady to receive it was the ballerina Dame Beryl Grey. Any foreign decoration has to be agreed by our Queen, and I was delighted to receive notification from Buckingham Palace saying that HM Queen Elizabeth II had agreed to the decoration being awarded to me. What an honour!

Chapter 19

DISCOVER DENMARK

Around the time of Sounds of Sweden, Denmark decided that they too would like a festival in England with the central focus on all six of the Nielsen symphonies. I was contacted by Jens Rossel from Copenhagen to ask if this Danish event could take place in Birmingham. Once again we had a meeting at Symphony Hall, with my now good friend Andrew Jowett. We had the embassy involved and Lyndon Jenkins from Symphony Hall.

The date was fixed from 6 October – 1 November 2001 and Annette Faaborg, Director of the Danish Information Centre, and I were appointed joint artistic directors. HRH Princess Alexandra of Denmark, wife of the Crown Prince of Denmark, and HRH The Duchess of Gloucester agreed to become Festival Patrons. The organising committee was Symphony Hall, The Royal Danish Embassy, Danish Secretariat For International Cultural Relations, Danish Music Information Centre and the Nordic Council of Ministers.

This was to be a longer event than Sounds of Sweden and was turning into an even bigger festival with much work to be done. I was pleased that I had an excellent team in the office and Martin Denny, by this time was a Director of my company Stephannie Williams Artists. Martin had to oversee work in the office when I was travelling either on the music cruises or with Lady Walton, or visiting Denmark. Martin was also very much involved with the organisation of Discover Denmark.

So it was decided that Discover Denmark was to be a month-long celebration with particular emphasis on Denmark's greatest composer Carl Nielsen. All his symphonies were to be performed, together with other important orchestral and choral works. Nielsen's last composition, the large-scale 'Commotio' was among the finest pieces of organ music composed in the last century and was to be played on Symphony Hall's new concert instrument, which would be inaugurated during the festival month.

Danish artists, orchestras and conductors took part and there were exhibitions, films and other associated events such as an International Carl Nielsen Symposium at Birmingham Conservatoire. This was the first major academic forum of its kind held outside Denmark, and attracted the world's leading Nielsen musicologists.

With such a huge and costly event, sponsorship or donations were needed to be found and we ended up with 49 sponsors or donors from participating organisations. This festival warranted a prestigious press launch but this time, instead of Andrew and Martin going to London to host and bring back to Birmingham the London press, a press launch was arranged in a restaurant in Tivoli Gardens, Copenhagen on 14 June.

The UK contingent was flown by courtesy of Maersk Air Ltd. Support for the launch came from the Danish Ministry of Foreign Affairs, Danish Tourist Board and Tivoli in association with the Danish Embassy in London. It was co-ordinated by Stephannie Williams Artists (SWA), Symphony Hall and the Danish Music Information Centre.

The UK guests were flown from Birmingham to Copenhagen and transported to Tivoli Gardens. These included, Andrew Jowett, from Symphony Hall, three Maersk Air Ltd representatives, myself with Madeleine from my company and five UK press, which included Christopher Morley, Chief Music Critic of the *Birmingham Post* and now my collaborator on this book.

We had a brilliant press launch, a meal in Glassalens Cafe in Tivoli Gardens, hosted by the Music Director of Tivoli, Lars Grunth, with whom I had worked on a number of occasions. Danish Radio was present and all the leading Danish press. That evening we were treated to a wonderful concert in the Tivoli Concert Hall given by the Tivoli Symphony Orchestra and the Copenhagen Royal Capella Choir, who my company happened to tour in the UK the following year.

We were taken from Copenhagen to Malmo, Sweden for our hotel accommodation. Malmo being just a short distance from Copenhagen, which took us over the sea by the Øresund Bridge, known as the Cultural Bridge. Next day we were transported back to Copenhagen for lunch aboard the famous galleon at Tivoli and our flight back to Birmingham.

Work now began in earnest, between cruises, other events and family commitments, on the festival arrangements, as we were bringing many artists and orchestras from Denmark to the UK.

In addition to music the festival included exhibitions about Carl Nielsen and his sculptress wife Anne Marie Carl-Nielsen, contemporary Danish, British and

Nordic Music, The International Carl Nielsen Symposium, Danish Design at the Birmingham Institute of Art & Design, and Danish Films at UGC Cinemas.

The Gala Opening was in the presence of HRH Princess Alexandra of Denmark and was given by the Tivoli Symphony Orchestra conducted by Giordano Bellincampi with Ingar Dam-Jensen, like Katarina Karneus from Sweden, another winner of the Cardiff Singer of the World competition, the Tivoli Guard and the Pantomime Ballet.

This was to provide a spectacular opener for the festival so I wanted it to include the composer Hans Christian Lumbye, known as the Danish Johann Strauss, who had also been responsible for the founding of the Tivoli concert series. A short piece by Nielsen was to be included as well as works by the Danish composer Niels Gade, Johann Strauss and Franz Lehár.

Lumbye's 'Copenhagen Steam Railway Galop' was included in the programme and I had heard that in Copenhagen's New Year Concert, they brought a miniature steam train onto the stage whenever this was performed. I thought this was a good idea so I asked Andrew if he would mind a miniature steam train coming onto the stage during the piece. He nearly fainted but said "if you can arrange it you can have it".

In the village of Wilmcote we had a railway enthusiast, Richard Perriam, and I went to consult him about the idea. It appeared he belonged to a miniature railway society and said he would discuss it with his fellow members and get back to me. There appeared to be no problem so we discussed details.

When the great day arrived the train enthusiasts turned up at Symphony Hall for the rehearsal with a miniature train. We decided that the 'Copenhagen Steam Railway Galop' should be first after the interval, as this would give them time to build the track. We rehearsed this with the Tivoli Orchestra conducted by Giordano, and decided when the train should appear with the whistle blowing. It all worked beautifully and everyone was excited about the forthcoming evening performance.

I was looking after Princess Alexandra that evening so I was sitting with her in the front of the circle. The first half of the concert went really well with the Pantomime Ballet dancing on the stage. The interval arrived and I took the Princess to the Green Room to be entertained by the dignitaries and then I departed to go backstage to check all was okay with the train. The track had already been built so we were all ready for the second half of the programme.

I made a speedy return to the Green Room to escort the Princess back to her seat. The 'Copenhagen Steam Railway Galop' started brilliantly and then it came to the point where the train should come in with a Dane sitting on it waving Danish flags. The train did not appear and I was getting concerned. I then saw Giordano looking in the wings probably saying to himself "where the devil is that train?!"

Halfway through the piece the train was sheepishly pushed onto the stage by the train enthusiasts. What a disappointment and embarrassment that was to me. Apparently an enthusiast had taken out one of the components because he thought it made it too noisy. He didn't think to try the train after removing it, but this stopped the train from going! I was very relieved that Chris Morley, writing a brilliant review of the concert that evening, very kindly omitted to mention the train incident!

Fortunately the rest of the concert continued without a hitch and Ingar Dam-Jensen sang Lehár songs beautifully. At the end of the programme the Tivoli Boys Guard marched onto the stage in full red uniform. The Tivoli Boys Guard was formed in 1868 and has its headquarters underneath the Tivoli Gardens. These boys are musically trained and march through the Tivoli Gardens for visitors, several times a week during the season. They are dressed in white trousers, a bright red jacket with brass trimmings and a busby on their heads.

It was quite a spectacle when 75 brilliant young musicians, all under fifteen, marched onto the stage playing superbly; it was quite a sight. Lumbye's 'Champagne Galop' completed the evening with champagne corks popping and audience reception at the end of the concert was very appreciative. It was a fantastic concert but the train incident remains one of the biggest disappointments of my career.

The Tivoli Symphony Orchestra is so named throughout the Summer months but, during the Winter and, when it tours, it is called the Copenhagen Philharmonic Orchestra. We called the orchestra Tivoli Symphony Orchestra for the Gala Opening Concert but the next night we called it the Copenhagen Philharmonic Orchestra and once again conducted by Bellincampi. It was an all Nielsen programme including the Violin Concerto played by Pekka Kuusisto, and the first of our Nielsen Symphonies to be performed in the festival.

The City of Birmingham Symphony Orchestra (Gwyn playing again) featured three of the symphonies, The Danish National Radio Symphony Orchestra performed one, and we entrusted the remaining symphony to the students of Birmingham Conservatoire. Conductors for these were Bellincampi, Sakari Oramo conducting two with CBSO and Ole Schmidt conducted the other, Andrew Mogrelia conducted the Birmingham Conservatoire Symphony Orchestra, and Gerd Albrecht conducted the Danish Radio Symphony Orchestra.

Other groups and performers in this festival were The Copenhagen Trio, which SWA had toured on many occasions; Birmingham Contemporary Music

Group; Birmingham Symphonic Winds; Athelas Sinfonietta Copenhagen; Anne Marie Abildskov, piano; Colin Parr, clarinet; Grethe Krogh, organ; Pierre-André Valade conductor; Jørgen Misser Jensen conductor; Keith Allen conductor; Christopher Austen conductor and Ebbe Munk conductor and director of the Copenhagen Royal Chapel Choir, which SWA was to tour the following year in the UK.

The music performed would be far too extensive to list but a tremendous amount of Carl Nielsen's music was heard during the month and given exposure to the British public. It was a very rewarding festival with which to be associated and received great media coverage, and strengthened links between Denmark and the UK.

St George's Chapel,
Windsor Castle.

Top left: Stephannie with Viking ship on River Avon. Built in one day by Stephannie and friends.
Top right: The author in the cloisters of Windsor Castle for the Garter Day ceremony.
Bottom: Stephannie meeting HRH The Prince of Wales.

Top (l-r): Lars Anders Tomter, Norwegian giant of the viola. Sigrun Edvaldsdottir, concert master of the Icelandic Symphony Orchestra; Tasmin Little (credit Benjamin Ealovega).

Middle (l-r): Vanya Milanova, Bulgarian violinist. Christopher Morley and Andrew Jowett, former director of Symphony Hall and Town Hall, Birmingham.

Bottom (l-r): Lady Susana Walton MBE. La Mortella. Sir Humphrey Burton.

Top (l-r): Daughter Kathryn's 18th birthday. Lucy aged 2 with Dan aged 6.

Middle (l-r): Stephannie with Dan playing the piano aged 2. Stephannie with her five youngest grandchildren.

Bottom (l-r): Stephannie in Copenhagen for launch of Discover Denmark. Revisiting Copenhagen with granddaughter Lucy.

Top: Christmas lunch – Stephannie's mother, Stephannie, Gwyn, Rosalind and Marjory.

Middle (l-r): Madelaine Newton, grandson Dan and Kevin Whately. Daughter Julia with grandchildren Dan and Lucy.

Bottom (l-r): Frances and Nick Bailey with grandson Henry, on a music cruise at Lake Bled, Slovenia. Daughter Rachel.

Top (l-r): Stephannie's Royal Order of the Polar Star. Elisabeth Soderstrom CBE. John Lill CBE.
Middle (l-r): Dame Felicity Lott. Launch of Discover Denmark in Tivoli Gardens, Copenhagen.
Bottom (l-r): John Wilson. The Copenhagen Trio.

Top (l-r): Maria Jagusz, mezzo soprano. Yvonne Howard, mezzo soprano.

Middle (l-r): Manaus Opera House in the middle of the Rain Forest in Brazil.
Brazilian boy with monkey on his head taken by Gwyn.

Bottom (l-r): Lady Walton at William's Rock. Susana Walton's ashes are also now buried in the
rock with William. Stephannie and Lady Walton going up the funicular to the swimming pool.

Top left: Gwyn and Stephannie in Egypt on a cruise.

Top right: Gwyn relaxing on a cruise.

Bottom: Gwyn and Stephannie on Adonia. Gwyn's last ever Music Festival at Sea in October 2014, eight months before he died. Photo taken by his friend Tom Collard.

Chapter 20

THE FIRST TWENTY YEARS OF MUSIC FESTIVALS AT SEA

In an earlier chapter I told the story of the first amazing Festival at Sea, at that time called Classical Music Cruises. Richard Baker did not like the title because he said this could put people off by thinking it was purely classical music. As we included lighter music, jazz, quizzes and talks it was not strictly classical music. It was Richard's idea to change the name to Music Festivals at Sea (MFAS). It took quite some time before P&O Cruises decided to change the name but by that time MFAS had become my second registered company at Companies House and I insisted this name be used for the music cruises.

Many things happened in the first twenty years and some exceptional artists were engaged. During these twenty years Richard was hosting the music cruises and we worked together planning artists and programmes. In a past chapter you will have heard how the music cruises started and the problems of the first cruise but through the years most of the problems were erased.

In the early days a number of artists were performing regularly such as Marilyn Hill Smith, Allan Schiller and the Coull Quartet, who we represented at that time. Although we had passengers' favourite artists returning, we never ever had the same team. This meant having different artists and a different combinations of instruments. I am proud to say that the programme content was never repeated in all the 35 years of MFAS.

On the first day of the cruise you never knew exactly how it would take off so this kept me on my toes. After the opening concert you got an idea which direction that particular cruise was going to take with different artists, different passengers, a different technical team and a different itinerary.

There were some funny questions asked in those early years. Philip Gallaway, violinist with the Coull Quartet informed me that he had been asked by a lady "Does it really matter where you put your fingers on the strings?" Another time, an elderly lady in the front row of a quartet concert, turned to her daughter and said in a loud voice "It is a very small quartet!"

On the first cruise we did not have a piano technician to tune the pianos but I found this essential so in future years a piano technician always travelled with us and tuned the pianos each day and was also on stand-by for any problems.

The pianos in those days were not very good and we had to make do with a small white Yamaha baby grand in the main concert venue, which was the cinema and another Yamaha in the International Lounge.

We were fortunate that one of our team was the very fine pianist Veronica McSwiney, who also happened to be married to the Captain, Chris Sample. Veronica was determined to get a good piano on the ship and discussed this with the Chairman of P&O Cruises, Lord Stirling. He gave her the authority to go to Steinway Hall to choose a piano for our concert venue so, thanks to Veronica we had a very splendid 'B' model Steinway piano in the cinema.

Having the Captain totally on our side was a great boon and the whole team were treated like royalty. At 12 noon there was always a noonday announcement, which went out all over the ship, giving passengers updated information on distances travelled etc. We had our morning concerts in the International Lounge and, as they started at 11am, there was always a danger that the announcement would disrupt the concert. However, Captain Sample said he would have the announcement isolated from the International Lounge but, to make sure it didn't happen, I was to run up to the bridge during the concert and remind the officer of the watch about isolating the noonday announcement from the venue.

On one particular occasion I ran up to the bridge as usual, and the nice young lad, Ian Hutley, on duty that day said "I know Stephannie – no noonday announcement". I went back to the concert reassured and, on that occasion we were running over time. At 12 noon our singer was in the middle of the beautiful Grieg song 'To the Spring' and suddenly the noonday announcement came through loud and clear with all the ship's information, plus an announcement that there would be fish & chips with mushy peas for lunch. We had to wait for this all to end and had to start the song again. I was furious and ran up to the bridge to tear a strip off the young Officer of the Watch. He apologised profusely but I was not happy.

Several years later I had heard that Ian had been promoted to Deputy Captain and a year later I was on the ship where he had been promoted as one of the youngest captains. At the Captain's Cocktail Party I bumped into Ian. He looked at me and said "Noonday announcement?" I felt rather embarrassed as I thought he must remember the ticking off I had given him but he continued with "I think I owe you something, would you like to bring your music team to the bridge for the sail away from Venice and I will even let you push the button for the horn to announce our departure". After this we got on very well.

I discovered Ian was a great Inspector Morse fan. On one occasion we had Janis Kelly on board, who sang all the songs in the series. Ian was participating in Desert Island Discs with Richard, and wanted 'Casta Diva' as his last choice, so we decided to drop a section of the stage down to the pit and hide the opening. We placed the piano with Michael Pollock at the piano and Janis next to him in Hawaiian costume, in the pit. As Ian announced his final choice, the stage came up from below with Janis singing 'Casta Diva'. This was a great surprise to everyone but a great thrill for Ian.

As I had worked in Scandinavia I was able to organise some events ashore. One was in Copenhagen when an open rehearsal was arranged in the Tivoli Concert Hall, with the Tivoli orchestra conducted by Kees Bakels. We were able to stay for part of the rehearsal and in the last piece the orchestra played a work by Lumbye, the Danish Johann Strauss, where all the cellos swivel their cellos round several times during the piece. This was a great thrill for the passengers.

We then went to eat in one of the many Tivoli restaurants. Following the meal we had arranged for the Glyptotek Museum to be opened especially for us on that day. We had a tour of the museum and then a recital with The Copenhagen Trio. The passengers loved the Trio and asked me if I could invite them for a future MFAS, which we did on many occasions.

On one cruise we had a young Tasmin Little, just starting out on her career as a violinist. On that cruise we had pianists Piers Lane, Michael Roll and David Pettit. We also had the brilliant Norwegian viola player Lars Anders Tomter, Angela Malsbury, clarinet, plus four fine singers. As part of the general entertainment P&O Cruises had engaged the pianist Bobby Crush as the cabaret artist. Bobby was an excellent pianist and when our team had a night off they all decided to go to Bobby's cabaret act.

For the last part of the act he asked the audience for requests and our team piped up with requests for Bach, a Rachmaninov prelude and a Chopin waltz.

Unfazed, he played everything that was requested and our team stood and cheered him at the end of the performance. Bobby was delighted that the music team turned up to support him and was pleased he could play all that was requested. Firm friendships were formed that night.

One of the very grand artists we had in the early days was the legendary tenor Nicolai Gedda. Working with Martin Martinsson in Sweden, we often talked about the music cruises and he asked me why I hadn't asked Gedda. I told him he must be joking because I would never get an artist as grand as Gedda. He said he thought he would enjoy it and gave me Gedda's number in Switzerland, where he spent half of the year. I decided to try and in trepidation I called the number. A deep voice answered and I asked to speak with Mr Gedda. He wanted to know who was speaking and what for. I told him who I was and that Martin Martinsson had given me the number. I went on to talk about the music cruise.

After I had finished speaking he said "I am Gedda, tell me more because I could be interested". I told him more but then added I hadn't got a huge fee and told him how much I could afford. In spite of the low fee he said he could be interested but he would like to join the ship in Travemunde and depart in Stockholm. This meant he would be on board for one week of the cruise, which was fine with me.

When we arrived in Travemunde, on that particular cruise, I was at the gangway to meet Gedda and his partner and take them to their very nice cabin. The first thing he wanted to do was to rehearse with the pianist, which on this occasion was Veronica McSwiney, Captain Sample's wife. Veronica was rather nervous about accompanying for such a star but they went off to rehearse on the Steinway in the cinema.

I went to see how they were getting on after an hour or so and found Gedda delighted with Veronica, saying she was a genius and he could not have had anyone better. That evening the Captain invited Gedda and partner, plus Richard and Margaret Baker and myself to dine at the Captain's table. Gedda was the life and soul of the party telling us many amazing stories. His recital was wonderful and he also gave an illustrated interview with Richard. On the day of his departure all the artists went down the gangway to see him off. A curtained black limo arrived to pick him up and he waved enthusiastically as he left the ship, with passengers on the decks waving back. What a thrill it was.

We started the music cruises on The Sea Princess, later to become the Victoria but then went on to the inaugural season on Oriana, followed by the inaugural season of Aurora, later the old Arcadia and then the new Arcadia. We had one cruise on Oceana but this did not work well for the music and neither did the New Arcadia. In addition to the bigger ships we were later given both Artemis and Adonia for our Music Festivals at Sea.

During the inaugural season of Oriana we had the film producer Ken Russell as one of the team. We thought it would be good to include some music films in the festival. We came up with the Ken Russell films of Elgar, The Boy Friend, the Tchaikovsky film (the Music Lovers) and Women in Love. To add to this we thought we should invite Ken to be interviewed by Richard prior to each film. I then went ahead and engaged Ken for this Oriana cruise.

The Cruise Director thought that the Women in Love would be a little too risqué for many passengers so it was agreed to show this at midnight. On that particular occasion there was a huge queue outside the Theatre Royal waiting for the doors to open. I was sitting behind a couple of elderly ladies. At the point in the film where Alan Bates and Oliver Reed were wrestling in the nude, in a large furnished room with log-burning fire, one of the ladies turned to the other and said "it is a very nice carpet dear!"

In the first twenty years artists included the Allegri, Vanbrugh, Chilingirian and Schidlof string quartets in addition to the Coull. Singers included John Mitchinson, Suzanne Murphy, Yvonne Howard, Bonaventura Bottone, Sally Burgess, Nicholas Folwell, Susanna Tudor Thomas, Anthony Kearns, Harry Nicoll, Ian Caddy, Jeremy Huw Williams, Janine Roebuck to name but a few. Peter Donohoe, Martin Roscoe, John Lenehan, Peter Katin and John Lill were pianists who performed during those first twenty years.

One of the popular pianists was John Lill who performed on the cruise on a number of occasions. It goes without saying that he was a brilliant pianist but he turned out to have a great sense of humour. The final concert of each cruise was called Homeward Bound and the artists performed spectacular pieces or fun pieces on this occasion. John asked me if he could perform his take-off of pianists for the last concert. I agreed thinking it would be famous classical pianists but he surprised us all. He played as Winifred Atwell, Scott Joplin, Liberace with the smile and even Semprini with spoken dialogue of ... "old ones, new ones, loved ones, neglected ones" just as Semprini had done in his programmes. It was a brilliant performance with all the above being played in the style of each pianist. John was loved by the passengers and artists alike.

It is impossible to tell all the stories or name all the wonderful artists involved because there were so many but they became part of our musical family and I have valued their continued friendship over the years.

The soprano Dame Felicity Lott remembers fondly her time as a performer on a Music Cruise:

"The cruise was memorable for several reasons. It was the first time Gabriel (my husband Gabriel Woolf, the actor) had ever done one, and we had no idea really of what to expect. I'll never forget heading for the theatre at one end of the ship before our first concert. We followed a man pushing his wife in a wheelchair, and she said loudly 'I hope

there won't be any bloody singers!' We recovered from that, but the sea was terribly rough and I had to hang onto the piano all through 'Vilia'; I don't think the piano was very stable either, so we probably waltzed together around the Bay of Biscay.

"Steve was smiling and imperturbable throughout … and there was quite a lot of 'out' to get through. We couldn't land at Gibraltar because someone was taken very ill and we had to make an earlier unscheduled stop to get him to hospital. That delayed us so we didn't see land for six days, and then it was in … Palma, possibly? which was closed on Sunday. We were supposed to go ashore on Corsica, but when the ship dropped its anchor it became detached, and divers had to be sent for to try to find it; meanwhile the ship wasn't stable enough to enable the tenders to leave safely.

"There seemed to be a series of marine disasters, but on the musical level there were some wonderful experiences. We made a lasting friendship with Danny Driver, and I heard Elgar's Piano Quintet for the first time in the Mediterranean; unforgettable. And Steve and Gwyn were always encouraging us and soothing our fragile egos!"

Chapter 21

THE NEXT FIFTEEN YEARS OF
MUSIC FESTIVALS AT SEA

As the next fifteen years evolved there were changes, and the major one was when Richard Baker decided he must ease out of hosting MFAS. This meant finding new presenters to follow Richard, which was not easy. At this stage, there were seven music cruises a year, and even eight in one year, so I was more at sea than at home. We felt it would be best to have a range of presenters. Previously Richard and I chose artists and worked on the programmes together, but now I was responsible for choosing, engaging artists and preparing the programmes.

Presenters

The first presenter following Richard was Henry Kelly, who was with Classic FM at that time. This was very much Richard's choice because I think he thought that Henry would take a different angle and this would be good. We then started to use other Classic FM presenters. Nick Bailey, the first voice of Classic FM Radio came next and has remained one of the mainstays ever since. Angela Rippon hosted one cruise and wore the most amazing dresses and shoes when presenting.

Humphrey Burton, who had been BBC Television's Head of Music and Arts, brought something different by including his talks on Leonard Bernstein, Yehudi Menuhin and William Walton. He had written books on these musicians and was a close friend of all three but especially to Bernstein.

Humphrey had produced programmes about Bernstein on BBC2, and the conductor/composer was so impressed with the results that he insisted on Humphrey being the producer for all his television work. This meant that all his presentations came from inside knowledge.

John Brunning and Anne-Marie Minhall joined the Classic FM line-up and were both excellent presenters. The actor Gabriel Woolf hosted one of the cruises. He is the husband of the wonderful soprano Dame Felicity Lott, who also joined that cruise and was a brilliant member of the team.

I remember there was a time we couldn't get into the port of Calvi due to bad weather. I had a call from the Cruise Director at around 7.30am to inform me we would not get into port that day so could I put on some extra entertainment. I said I could provide a quiz myself but I would call the artists together and devise a programme.

The artists arrived in my cabin shortly after the call and I explained the situation. Flott, as we called Felicity, quickly piped up with "I can do a recital this afternoon, if Terry is happy", Terry Albright being the pianist on that occasion. He readily agreed, so it was decided we should present a Celebrity Recital that afternoon, after I had hosted a quiz in the morning. Other entertainers on board were also doing their bit, so nothing else was needed to be provided by the music team.

The Cruise Director was duly informed and within an hour a programme of events was printed and delivered to all the passengers' cabins informing them of the events that had been arranged, due to the cancellation of the visit to Calvi.

Concerts Ashore

Besides the Copenhagen trip already mentioned we started to give more concerts ashore, when in certain ports. This was very rewarding because in the venues chosen no amplification was needed and we could produce a pure acoustic sound.

There were a few favourite places, where we visited regularly and presented concerts. One of these was the monastery in Valldemossa, Majorca, Spain. This is where Chopin spent a winter with his partner George Sand and subsequently this was made into a museum with a large collection of Chopin memorabilia, including the Pleyel piano that Chopin had transported from France for him to use for his composing.

Unfortunately the wet and cold winter climate was not good for the consumption from which he was suffering, so they left after spending only one winter there. The monastery is now open to visitors and there is a beautiful small concert room, with stage and grand piano, attached to the monastery with magnificent paintings on the walls and ceilings. A Chopin festival is held there every year so, I thought a tour from the ship to the monastery and then a recital in the Concert Hall would be perfect.

We have had many fine pianists playing on these trips including Martin Roscoe, Danny Driver, Cristiano Burato, Katya Apekisheva, Julian Jacobson, Morten

Mogensen, and John Wilson to name but a few. John also gave a recital with Maria Jagusz singing some of the Chopin songs in Polish. This trip was very popular and always sold out as tickets were limited due to the size of the concert hall.

Another popular trip was to Grieg's house in Troldhaugen. Having worked in Norway I was able to get it booked at a very low rent for a concert. A tour of the house and garden was given to the passengers including seeing the little hut where Grieg composed. With him being a very small man it was interesting to see that the piano stool had been raised by a couple of volumes of Beethoven sonatas. The concert hall was acoustically magnificent and housed a beautiful model 'D' Steinway grand piano. The raked seating went down to a stage that had full length picture windows looking out over the fjord.

The artists loved performing there and we had a wide range of them giving recitals of Grieg's music. We had piano, violin and piano or voice and piano recitals and on one occasion we took the Con Tempo Quartet to perform one of Grieg's string quartets. One popular piece played was 'Wedding Day at Troldhaugen', and it was wonderful to think this is where it had been composed and was performed by Grieg for his wife Nina to celebrate their 25th wedding anniversary.

I had known the curator of the house, Erling Dahl but, unfortunately, when he left, the house was taken over by a committee and the hire fee went up so much we were unable to afford the trip anymore. Not to be outdone I decided to investigate the possibility of going to Ole Bull's house. Ole Bull was a friend of the Grieg family and was a very famous Norwegian violinist and composer. According to Robert Schumann he was on a level with the great Paganini.

Ole Bull could be described as the Norwegian 'pop' star of the day. He undertook a tour of the USA and, on his return, bought Lysøen, The Island of Light, with his earnings from the tour. The next year he undertook a second tour of the States and, on his return this time, he built a magnificent villa with the money. The house is now a museum and has a lovely concert hall built into the house.

I made contact with the curator, who was delighted that I wanted to take passengers to the house. I asked if we could take a violinist and pianist to give a concert. Unfortunately the piano at the house was not in good condition so could not be played but we could give a solo violin recital. Kerenza Peacock was our violinist on that cruise and was excited at the thought of performing on Lysøen. She was even more delighted when the curator said that she could perform on Ole Bull's Guarnerius Violin, which was kept in a glass cabinet.

We had two coaches booked for the concert and then we had two boats to take passengers over to the Island. The concert hall could only take one coach load at a time so one party was taken for a tour of the house and given coffee and waffles. This was then reversed so everyone had a chance to hear the recital. Kerenza excelled herself as she had read up about Ole Bull and was able to give the passengers a short talk before performing on his very rare instrument. She performed unaccompanied Bach and Paganini besides a few of Ole Bull's own compositions.

Other concerts ashore included the Manuel Theatre, a baroque theatre in Valletta, the capital of Malta. On that cruise we had Charles and Ingrid Medlam, founders of London Baroque, who brought on the cruise their viola d'amore, viola da gamba and a harpsichord. Charles and Ingrid were able to take their instruments, together with our lovely mezzo soprano Yvonne Howard to give a baroque concert. Bob Glazebrook, ex-managing director of Steinway, was our piano technician on that occasion and he was able to tune the harpsichord.

We were told a vehicle would be sent to transport the harpsichord. When it arrived, to our horror, it turned out to be an open-back little truck. We did not think we could send a valuable harpsichord off in the truck. Bob solved the problem and said "we shall put the harpsichord into the truck, cover it and tie it down, and then I shall travel with it holding on to it to make sure it is okay". What a sight that was to see the ex-managing director of Steinway, standing in the back of the truck holding the harpsichord, as they drove off through the town!

Another experience and another great concert.

Other music tours went to the Mascagni museum in Livorno, Italy, the Svenska Rikskonserter Concert Hall in Stockholm, through my Swedish connections, another baroque concert in Rostock, Germany with all the Medlam family i.e. Charles, Ingrid and their two children Lukas and Hannah Medlam. Lukas and Hannah are now making a name for themselves in the music profession.

It is also worth mentioning Varna in Bulgaria because, through our lovely violinist Vanya Milanova, we were able to engage her father's large, spectacular folk group singing, dancing and performing on their instruments, wearing the most magnificent hand-embroidered costumes.

Our Baltic Cruise took us to Odessa and here there was a surprise concert for Gwyn and myself! We arrived in Odessa, Ukraine, at about 8am but as I had work to do I did not leave the ship until approx. 10am. As I came down the gangway Gwyn said "there are some people over there and they have a sign up with your name on it". I said it couldn't be me because I didn't know anyone here. We decided to go over to the lady and two men waiting there. Sure enough they were waiting for me and wanted to take us to the Odessa music school. Reluctantly we got into their vehicle and were transported to the music school.

When we arrived we were taken up a grand staircase in need of repair but with a magnificent picture of the renowned violinist David Oistrakh facing us. It appeared he had been a great teacher at this school, as was the eminent pianist, Emil Gilels. We were then led into a large room where students were waiting to perform for us. They were all dressed in black and white concert dress and had obviously been awaiting our arrival for a couple of hours. They gave us an outstanding concert but we were shocked to see that they had no music stands and their music was photocopied sheets, which they read from the floor. The instruments were not in good condition but these brilliant young musicians made a great sound. We were very humbled by this experience.

I do not know to this day how they got my name or even knew I was on the ship, but they wanted to tell me how desperate they were for music and equipment since the end of Communism. They wanted to know if, when we visited again, we could take things for them. Gwyn and I were very moved by this visit. The following year we returned to Odessa and went laden with music, strings, music stands and even a set of piano strings donated by Bob Glazebrook.

Gwyn and I had been gathering all this material from friends, and some of the musicians from the ship wanted to come with us and donate music. Richard Baker also came and made a speech with our donation. The appreciation was immeasurable and we felt thrilled that we were able to do something for these talented young musicians.

Another memorable event was in Reykjavik. Once again I was very fortunate to have contacts, due to my representation of Sigrún Eðvaldsdóttir, now concertmaster of the Iceland Symphony Orchestra. Through Sigrún I had been invited to meet the Icelandic Ambassador in London, Helgi Augusston and his lovely wife Heba. I got advice from the Icelandic Embassy on what I could do with a music tour in Reykjavik.

I was introduced to one of the best choral directors in Iceland, Thorgerdur Ingolfsdottir, and she agreed to her young choir singing in the Perlan Restaurant. The restaurant was built over a geyser and was on the top floor, where the geyser rose up every few minutes through a central glass casing. It was amazing to see and the restaurant was superb. I think the fish I had there was the nicest I have ever tasted.

On the day of the trip we arrived at the restaurant for lunch and the Foreign Minister's wife was there to greet us and join us. At the end of the meal the choir of young men and girls entered in full Icelandic costume singing in harmony. It was a wonderful choir and then, yet another treat, the superb Icelandic bass-baritone, Sigur Bragasson sang some beautiful solos for us. It was an incredible concert.

Following the concert there was another treat in store for us. The Foreign Minister's wife joined our coach party go to The White House, where the 1986 Reykjavik Summit meeting was held when President Ronald Reagan of the USA and Mikhail Gorbachev of the USSR discussed the ending of the Cold War at that time.

Our party was greeted with a glass of sherry and then given a tour of the house. The P&O Captain on our ship was Michael Moulin and, in return for the Icelandic hospitality he invited Icelandic dignitaries to a reception on the ship prior to our sailing away.

Manaus Opera House

This needs a special mention as it was yet another unforgettable experience.

Music Festivals At Sea was engaged for a six week cruise up the Amazon on the P&O ship Artemis. The ship would sail from Southampton to a few ports in the Caribbean and then on to the Amazon, where we would sail up to Manaus with a few stops on the way. This needed careful planning because we had to sustain the quality of performance for six weeks. We had three different presenters and they were Richard Baker for the first two weeks, Humphrey Burton for the next two weeks and Nick Bailey for the final two weeks.

It was a great team and included Ingrid Surgenor, David Pettit and Cristiano Burato as the pianists with Patrick Healy as choral director. Angela Malsbury clarinet and Mara Martinelli flute, Peter Thomas, violin, Hans Nygaard, cello, plus a few other instrumentalists, and a wide range of music was performed on that cruise. The highlight of that cruise was to be the concert in the Manaus Opera House and the second highlight was the passenger performance of 'The Pirates of Penzance'.

I desperately wanted to give a concert in the Manaus Opera House, where the great Caruso had sung. However, I was told that it was very difficult dealing with Brazilians because of the language. I had recently been introduced to a very fine Brazilian guitarist Fabio Zanon and thought it would be good to have a Brazilian, who spoke excellent English, as one of our team. I then discovered his fiancée was the daughter of the then Brazilian Ambassador in London.

I managed to get myself introduced to the Brazilian Embassy and discussed the possibility of using the Manaus Opera House on our Brazilian trip. I was told to leave it to them and the Embassy would sort it all for me, which they did. Both Fabio and Marianne, his fiancée, acted as interpreters for us.

On the day of the Manaus Opera House concert, the ship was running late, due to the dodgy tides. We should have arrived in the afternoon but, in the event, we didn't arrive until 9.30pm. The concert had been scheduled for 7.30pm! This put great pressure on our four singers Marilyn Hill Smith, Janine Roebuck, Gwyn Hughes Jones, Ian Caddy and of course our pianist Ingrid Surgenor.

The excellent Purser at that time Zak Coombs, suggested that I get my team ready in evening dress, ready to leave the ship as soon as we docked, and as soon as the gangway went down. We were all ready at the top of the gangway by 9.30pm and, as soon as the gangway went down we departed the ship and boarded the coach waiting to take us to the opera house. What we had not expected was to see a large crowd of Brazilians watching the ship dock and then watching, with amazement, this finely dressed group leaving the ship and boarding the coach.

On arrival at the opera house we were shown onto the stage for our necessary rehearsal. We were pleased that we had taken our medication for malaria because there were large mosquitoes flying around the lights on the stage. The Opera House was built at the time of the wealthy rubber barons and no expense had been spared. The auditorium had marble pillars and a great deal of Murano glass brought from Venice. In the centre of the auditorium, if you looked up at the dome, it was a replica of the Eiffel Tower so it appeared you were standing under the Eiffel Tower.

It was now time for the very short rehearsal and we were so pleased to have Fabio and Marianne as our interpreters. Fabio dealt with the stage staff and Marianne with the lighting, above and at the back of the hall. We had taken our piano technician with us, even though we had been told the piano had been tuned that morning. Ingrid sat at the piano and started to play but soon stopped and said "this piano is terribly out of tune". I then decided the rehearsal would have to wait because the tuning of the piano was more important. By this time it was nearly 10.30pm and although the passengers had been told that the concert would be delayed until 11pm it didn't give us much time for rehearsing.

Alex, our tuner, got cracking on the piano but the guests had started to arrive. They were being given champagne and canapes in the foyer but I knew we had to have a short rehearsal so the singers could get the feel of the hall. I told Alex he would have to stop tuning shortly. He look at Ingrid and said "I've done the middle but only have time for the top or bottom, what do you want Ingrid, the treble or the bass?" She replied "I'll take the treble!" We only had time for a very short rehearsal before the guests entered the theatre, but it was a tremendous concert with the artists performing to a totally full opera house. I don't think there were many passengers left on the ship that night.

We sailed the Amazon on a few subsequent occasions and it was always a great thrill for our singers to perform in this amazing opera house. All the staff at the theatre came to know me, so it became easier each time.

Productions

Around the year 2000, through Linda Ormiston and Kathryn Harries we launched the concept of productions with passengers. When Linda and Kathryn were on board, as part of the team, they thought it would be good to work together with the passengers on presenting 'HMS Pinafore' by Gilbert and Sullivan. I thought it was a great idea but I told them we didn't have the music. Linda had a vocal score with her and she said, if she could use the photocopier, she would spend the night copying the music for the passengers.

Linda was as good as her word and the next day, all the passengers had copies of 'HMS Pinafore'. Linda played the piano for rehearsal and both Linda and Kathryn took the choir practices. By the end of the cruise the choir had made such good progress, it was decided to perform the work for fellow-passengers. David Pettit agreed to play the piano for the performance and Linda conducted. Between them Linda and Kathryn played all the solo roles, changing hats for each different character. It was such a success that future choral works were planned on the longer cruises.

Rehearsals were built into the programme of events and it was decided we would have a choral director plus four singers, in addition to the instrumentalists, whenever we had choral cruises. Over the years there have been many G&S performances of 'The Mikado', 'HMS Pinafore', 'The Pirates of Penzance' and 'Trial by Jury', and had some excellent choral directors, including Patrick Healy, Robert Dean, Jeffrey Howard and Jeremy Silver.

It was especially good when we could include members from the show company and cabaret artists in the productions. This brought a feeling of togetherness around the ship and the show company members could sing and dance. Having the Captain playing a role was also a bonus. With 'HMS Pinafore' we were able to include the boys from the Headliners Show Company dressed as sailors dancing the Sailor's Hornpipe. When we needed more than four solo singers in a production we were able to use a show company singer. Bruce Morrison was Production Manager for the Headliners and, on one occasion we needed a Pirate King so he stepped in and did a grand job for us.

I was in trouble on one of the cruises, and this was due to Patrick Healy! We were in Rhodes at the time, and we passed a shop where they had pistols in the window. Patrick said that as the pistol was only 18 euros I should buy it because it would be perfect for the Pirate King, who happened to be Bruce. I took some persuading but eventually agreed to buy the pistol. It was wrapped into newspaper for me and put into a bag.

On arriving back at the ship I put my pistol through the security machine and a terrified Indian officer said "who does this gun belong to?" "It belongs to me," I piped up and then continued, "it's for the Pirate King in The Pirates of Penzance". Of course he had no idea what I was talking about, but quickly said "I shall have to give this to the security officer and he will be in touch with you". I knew Malcolm, the Security Officer and was not surprised when he called me.

I explained how I had got the pistol and what it was for. He said that was fine but he would hold on to it and give it to me for rehearsals and the performance but, other than that he would keep it. I discovered later that it was a cigarette lighter and Malcolm was using it to light his cigarettes!

There are many more stories of productions but far too many to tell here.

In addition to G&S productions we found that oratorios with passengers were also very popular, and we worked on a number of Messiah performances, Haydn's 'Creation', Vivaldi's 'Gloria' and the Fauré 'Requiem'. Haydn's 'Creation' was a spectacular performance conducted by John Bethell. We had a recording of the overture and, in consultation with the Production Manager, we had the stage in darkness for the recorded overture and, as the overture was coming to an end the lights gradually came up, but with dry ice so there appeared to be clouds on the stage and as the light became clearer John, the conductor, was standing on the rostrum in his tailsuit, and it could have been God appearing at the beginning of the world.

Many of these productions would not have been possible without the brilliant technical teams on the ships. One Production Manager always went that extra mile for us to make a spectacular presentation and that was Chris Bullock. He and his team gave us the most wonderful sets for all our performances and made sure the sound and lighting was the best we could possibly get. Some of the productions turned out to be like West End shows, especially when we started to acquire costumes.

Dorothy Collard was our wardrobe mistress. Being a member of the Havant Operatic Society, and having sung in many G&S performances, she became very much involved with our productions. She had come onto a cruise for the first time with her husband Tom as a passenger, after having had a serious cancer operation. On this cruise we didn't have a Ruth for our 'Pirates' production so she stepped in and sang the role brilliantly.

After that Tom and Dorothy sailed frequently on the music cruises and then took charge of costumes. Having a large farmhouse, Dorothy was not only able to store our costumes, but also a number she had acquired from various operatic societies. Tom was also a tremendous help with productions and made various 'props' when required, such as truncheons for the policemen in 'Pirates'. There were quite a few passengers who became very much involved with the music cruises, and every cruise was like another huge party with friends.

Innovations and happenings

One really good addition to the music cruise was having the percussion group Maraca2 join the team. The members of Maraca2 were Tim Palmer and Jason Huxtable. It took some planning because they boarded the ship with a van-load of percussion instruments that had to be stored on the ship, and also they needed somewhere to rehearse. We ended up giving them the orchestra pit for rehearsals, as this was the only place big enough to house all the instruments, which included two marimbas.

Besides virtuoso concerts on percussion instruments they gave a demonstration concert, where passengers were invited to play various instruments, in a performance of Ravel's 'Bolero'. When we were in child-friendly ships Tim and Jason gave workshops to the children and then had them all performing at the end of the cruise. Another innovation with Maraca2 was handbell ringing. This was on a cruise near to Christmas and the boys brought a box of handbells with them onto the ship. The passengers ended up playing Christmas Carols at the end of the cruise.

It was always good to involve children in the MFAS, if there were any on board, and we did have a few really exciting concerts with children, not least a few using Saint-Saens' 'Carnival of the Animals'. One of our artists, usually John Wilson, by this time our pianist-in-residence, arranged the work for all the instruments we had on board. The children in Peter Pan's or Jumping Jack's children's areas would spend part of the cruise drawing big pictures of the animals. On the day of the concert, which was usually at the end of the cruise, the children would join the instrumentalists and the narrator on stage.

One performance of this was superbly narrated by Kevin Whately, who, having grandchildren of his own, was very good with the little children sitting on cushions at the front of the stage. He was left in charge of the children as well as narrating the story! As each animal was performed by the professionals, a picture of the animal was depicted on the side screens and the child, with that animal, stood up with the picture, displaying it to the audience. It was inevitable that some of the children wanted to wave to their parents and got distracted from the job they were doing. One little girl held up her picture but was more interested in pulling up her knickers, which were falling down!

The children were fascinated by the live music being performed on stage and some wanted to move themselves closer to the artists to get a better look! What a thrill it was for the children to be involved and to experience live music in this way. It is a pity we later only worked on child-free ships, as we had so much to offer the children from tinies up to teenagers.

One year we had a number of artists' very musical children on board. These were Hannah and Lukas Medlam, mentioned before, but then only 14 and 16, plus the daughter of Paul Barritt our violinist, the daughter of Imoko Imai, the viola player and James Lisney's daughters Emma and Joy only four and six at the time. We decided to give a concert with all these children in the main theatre.

It was a capacity audience, and the children received a well-deserved standing ovation. This was not surprising with some of the music performed, including Lukas playing Wienawski on the violin and Hannah performing Chopin's 'Fantasie-Impromptu'. The concert ended with Hannah on the piano, Lukas on violin and six-year-old Joy on cello giving a superb performance of Haydn's 'Gypsy Rondo Trio'.

It is not surprising that this concert still remains in many people's memory.

You can't do 35 years of music cruises on ships without having a few mishaps, and there were several occasions when the pianos slid off the stage in bad weather.

One occasion was when Peter Donohoe was on board. We were in the International Lounge rehearsing for a Music in the Morning programme. The piano was standing in the middle of the stage, fortunately no one playing at the time, but there was a sudden lurch from a huge wave and the piano took off, went over the edge of the stage and landed in four seats in the front row. Fortunately there was no audience at that time.

The stage lads lifted the piano back onto the stage and we looked at the damage done. It seemed okay apart from the fact that the pedals had bent. Peter kicked them back in place and said "tie it up and it will be okay". We gave the concert with the piano roped to a post at the side of the stage. Some of the artists felt queasy and had a job standing to perform, but they all took part in the concert, even Marilyn Hill Smith, who, between numbers, was running off to be sick and then coming back again for her next song.

On one occasion in bad weather Sigrún Eðvaldsdóttir, the Icelandic violinist and David Pettit, piano, gave a recital which included the Cesar Franck sonata. The piano was once again roped to the side of the stage. We gave Sigrún a stool so she could sit to play but she ignored this and went onto the stage, looked at the audience and said "don't mind me, my father's a fisherman".

There were of course occasions when artists were sick and unable to perform, so programmes had to be rearranged, and naturally this was my responsibility. On one occasion our tenor lost his voice but only decided a couple of hours before the Gala Opera Night that he would be unable to sing. This meant our skipping dinner and getting the singers and pianist together to rehearse a different programme. As all the artists were so professional (I think the pianist on this occasion was the wonderful Michael Pollock), it all worked well. An amazing Gala Opera performance was given and most passengers were unaware we were a tenor missing.

Duo Concerts

On one cruise I was fortunate to have three pianists, one being Michael Pollock a brilliant repetiteur, and the other two were Leeds International prize winners. These were Cristiano Burato and Katya Apekisheva. I was told it would not be good to have these two pianists on together, but I decided Katya's recital, as she was Russian, would be Mussorgsky's 'Pictures at an Exhibition'. Cristiano, an Italian but a Chopin specialist would give a Chopin recital. This worked well, and I found the two became great friends on the cruise.

During Katya's recital of 'Pictures at an Exhibition' a string broke in the bass of the piano. At the time she was playing 'Baba Yaga', which is a very flashy movement of the piece. Katya struggled on for a few minutes and then stopped and said "sorry, I can't play any more," Cristiano, who was in the audience, leapt up from his seat, then ran and jumped onto the stage and pulled out the rattling string, looked at Katya and said "now carry on". The ovation for both at the end of the piece was incredible.

As these two fine pianists were on board at the same time it seemed obvious to give them a duet recital. This was a spine-tingling experience and people would have been prepared to pay a great deal to hear these two great artists performing together.

Another duo recital, which was memorable, especially to me, was when we had the sponsorship of two Yamaha handmade grand pianos so that we could include two duo concerts with Peter Donohoe and Martin Roscoe. The pianos were craned onto the ship at the start of the cruise. This had never been done before and it caused quite a stir, enough of a stir to get the media interested in using this as a news story.

The concert was a very virtuosic affair, including Stravinsky's 'Petrushka'. Elaine Burns, Peter's wife, was turning the pages for Martin and I was turning the pages for Peter. Just before going onto the stage Peter said "oh, by the way there is a six page turn-back at the beginning of the first piece". I replied "great!"

We all went onto the stage of a crowded Princess Theatre. The piece started and Peter turned to me and muttered something, which I could not hear. He repeated it again but I still could not hear so he said in a very loud voice audible to the whole theatre "we're not going to do the six page turn-back after all!"

The other amazing duo performance on a ship was with John Wilson and his talented pupil Nicholas Rimmer, now in great demand internationally as pianist and conductor. It was on the ship Artemis, and we were very fortunate to have two Steinway pianos on board. One of the pianos was a new Steinway, chosen at Steinway Hall by Bob Glazebrook, retired Managing Director of Steinway, especially for the MFAS. There was a piano in the International Lounge and another at the extreme opposite end of the ship, in the Starlight Lounge.

We had the crazy idea of bringing these two pianos together for a duo concert but this was not easy on a ship as both pianos were used daily. The other reason was that it could be dangerous to move a grand piano with so many passengers around. The night before the concert we gathered together the production team into the Starlight Lounge at midnight. We had John Anstey, our Steinway technician, with us at the time, so he removed the legs and had the piano wrapped in a blanket, and was there to supervise operations. He had fortunately brought the piano-moving wheels on board for this exercise.

The piano was gently lifted onto the wheels and eight young lads, with John watching over them, moved the piano along the open deck all the way to the International Lounge. The same operation had to be done the following night, after the concert, to get it back in position for the next day's events. It was all worthwhile because an outstanding programme was given by John and Nicholas, which included a two-piano version of music from the opera 'Carmen', which had been arranged by John.

These are just a few of the tales I have to tell of spending almost half my life at sea!

Although, like Nelson, I have never been a good sailor, over the years I have managed to control the mal de mer and have never missed a rehearsal or concert.

Margaret Baker said to me one day "Why do you have to attend every concert?" I replied "because it is my job and, anyway, a string could break". She quickly came back with "and what do you think you could do about it?"

Shortly after this we were sitting together during a concert and Paul Barritt was playing the flashy piece 'Banjo & Fiddle', when suddenly his e string broke. Margaret turned to me and said "there you are, what are you going to do about it?" I needn't have worried because Paul dashed off the stage, changed the string and came back to play the piece all over again. Richard Baker was so good in these instances because he would take to the stage and tell one of his very amusing anecdotes. We all worked together as a team.

It has been a joy working on so many P&O ships, with the P&O ship's company, production teams and working with so many very fine artists. Besides international artists we have had young musicians starting out on their careers but who are now of international renown. From the thousands of passengers I have gained many lifelong friends.

Chris and Carole Hancock arranged a memorable surprise for me on the 25th Anniversary Music Cruise, when they organised their fellow-passengers to contribute towards a beautiful commemorative silver medal. Chris had this specially made in Birmingham's Jewellery Quarter, and P&O Cruises gave permission for their colours to be used on the ribbon.

Being able to have Gwyn with me, once he retired, not only as my partner but as an artist performing in many concerts was very good. It was a bonus having a viola player because he could join other artists in chamber works such as viola quintets, the Mozart Kegelstatt Trio with clarinet, viola and piano, and also the Brahms songs for mezzo, piano and viola, which he frequently performed with Yvonne Howard or Maria Jagusz. In addition he played many solos on board and stood in on the occasion when foreign artists could not get to the ship, due to the ash cloud incident in Iceland.

I was very fortunate that I was also able to take my girls on board in the early days when the cruises were in holiday time, and later on all the grandchildren have experienced life at sea on Nanny's ships, as they call them! What a wonderful thirty-five years it has been.

Chapter 22

GWYN

One of the last photographs of Gwyn on his final music cruise, taken by his friend Tom Collard.

At the end of January 2012 our life changed. Gwyn was diagnosed with cancer of the larynx. He had to have 35 days of radiotherapy, plus chemotherapy once a week. This meant daily visits to Coventry University Hospital for many weeks. The treatment was very unpleasant but Gwyn kept smiling, as he always did, and tried to live as normal a life as possible, even though the treatment was unpleasant; he became very tired throughout and was relieved when it came to an end.

We then had monthly check-ups with the oncologist at Coventry Hospital. All seemed to be going well and Gwyn continued to live his life to the full. Unfortunately, almost a year later the cancer returned and Gwyn was told that the larynx had to be removed, which meant he would need a speech valve. It was a long operation but, as always, he bounced back and got to grips with learning how to speak with pressing the valve.

Once again he was determined to live life to the full and even came on the cruises with me. Fortunately I learnt how to change his valve whenever necessary and it was good to have him travelling with me. On one of the cruises we were at the top of Norway and went into a supermarket to buy a few things. A beautiful young, blonde Norwegian girl was at the checkout. When she told us the price Gwyn pressed his valve and said "how much?!" The girl looked at him and said "what's that?", pointing to the valve. Gwyn replied "I'm a Dalek!" The young girl looked in admiration and said "that's cool!" Back on the ship Gwyn told everyone how a beautiful young Norwegian girl thought he was cool! Gwyn always had a great sense of humour.

There were a number of cruises with Gwyn joining me but now not performing. All seemed to be going well with the regular check-ups at Coventry Hospital but then, what we dreaded happened: in October 2013 the cancer returned. The surgeon who had performed the earlier operation was reluctant to operate this time because there was a risk of damaging a nerve to the spine or brain and then Gwyn's quality of life would be very limited.

Gwyn decided he didn't want the operation but our lovely MacMillan nurse, Mary, suggested we sought a second opinion. Without much confidence we agreed to her investigating possibilities. This was on a Monday and on the Tuesday Mary called to say Mr Clarke, a specialist in his field, had a clinic the next day at Charing Cross Hospital in London. She asked if we could get there for 10.30am but we might have to wait several hours as we were being slotted in. Mr Clarke worked at the Royal Marsden, Harley Street and Charing Cross Hospital. It was a stroke of luck he happened to be at Charing Cross the next day. Without hesitation we said we would be there.

We arrived at the hospital in plenty of time for the 10.30am appointment, expecting to wait for hours but, after approximately an hour Mr Clarke came out himself and called for Gwyn Williams. In trepidation we went into the little cubicle with him and waited to hear what he would say.

He said he had looked at the scans and the biopsy and had decided what he would do. He went on to explain in great detail the long operation that would take place, together with his plastic surgeon colleague. I then said that Mr Tedla in Coventry was worried about performing such an operation due to the risks involved. "I'm not worried about that, I have done many of these operations!" he abruptly told us. I then went on to ask how long Gwyn would have if the operation was not performed. He said Gwyn would have three months at the most.

He went on to say that he could not promise it would be a success, because sometimes things slipped through, but he would whip out everything possible and give Gwyn another six months at least. As it happened he gave him another eighteen months.

We immediately said we wanted to go ahead with the operation but he thought it would be good for us to go and have a coffee and return an hour later to let him know what we had decided to do. If we went ahead we would then be seen by the plastic surgeon, who would explain his part in the operation.

We went to have our coffee and discussed this new turn of events, which we could not believe. Very excitedly we went back to the waiting-room and were shortly seen by the plastic surgeon, who gave us all his side of the procedure. We knew it would be a very long operation and we were told we had to wait until these two great men would be free to undertake this long complicated operation.

The date was fixed for Tuesday 26 November 2013. We had to be at the hospital by 7.30am. Julia wanted to be with me throughout the operation, and we had booked into a nearby hotel as we knew we would have a long agonising wait. I'm not sure how we lived through that day but we tried to keep ourselves occupied, holding hands, and it was so good to have Julia with me. Gwyn went into the operating theatre at 9.30am and came out of the theatre just after 9.30pm. Julia was determined to stay with me until Gwyn came round so we comforted each other.

It was an horrendous operation and that night Gwyn was not really with us, but the next morning he was awake and smiling as he always was. Julia reluctantly went home that day but I stayed at the hotel for the weeks Gwyn was in hospital in London so that I could be there for him every day. Some of our wonderful London friends visited him. One of the visitors was our lovely friend Yvonne Howard. I should also mention that, from the time Gwyn was diagnosed, Yvonne sent him a text message every day, from wherever she was performing throughout the world. This meant a great deal to Gwyn and also to me because I knew what a true friend she was.

Whenever Yvonne visited she took me out for a meal following the visit. Other friends visiting apart from our family were John and Linda Anstey, our cruise piano technician and his wife, Classic FM's Nick Bailey, the viola player John Brearley, the double-bass player David Jones, Classic FM's John Brunning and many more of our musical friends.

Gwyn came out of hospital just in time for Christmas. On discharge day, Rachel got someone to look after her five children and drove to the hospital from Wallingford early in the morning. Unfortunately Gwyn was not discharged until later that day so Rachel had the long drive back with us to Stratford in the rush hour. We were all so relieved to have him home.

Although Gwyn was finding difficulty eating, all the family celebrated Christmas together and thanked the lord for Gwyn's recovery from such an ordeal. Throughout the year Gwyn was progressing well and said he would come on the October 2014 cruise with me. This was the 30th anniversary cruise of Music Festivals at Sea and it was to be a very special cruise, because we knew so many of our friends of the MFAS had booked to be with us to celebrate. This cruise was on the smaller P&O ship Adonia.

The night before the cruise we had our cases packed and labelled in the hall ready for take-off and I noticed Gwyn had put his viola case with the other cases. Knowing he had not played the viola for three years I enquired, "why are you taking your viola on this cruise?" His reply, "I'm taking it but I'm not saying I'm playing".

We had been given a lovely suite on this Adonia cruise to the Baltic. We settled into the suite and then I left Gwyn to rest while I went to check all the arrangements and visit the artists in their cabins. Nick Bailey was host on this cruise and we had John Wilson and Michael Pollock pianos, Sarah Helsby-Hughes soprano, Yvonne Howard mezzo, John Hudson tenor, Arwel Huw Morgan bass-baritone and the ConTempo String Quartet, the Romanian quartet-in-residence for RTE radio and television. What I could call my dream team. On my return to the cabin Gwyn was practising. I was very surprised but he again told me he was not saying he would play on the cruise.

On the first evening at sea I have all the artists in my cabin to meet each other, have a glass of wine and then discuss the forthcoming events. We discussed the events for the first day at sea and then I wanted to check the programme for the first Music In The Morning. I went round all the artists checking their items and, as I reached the last item, Gwyn spoke up with his valve "and I shall perform 'Rosie's Tune'." This was a piece John Wilson had composed for a little girl viola player but had brought to our house for Gwyn to play because it was too advanced, at this stage, for the young girl. Gwyn had been the only person to perform this piece.

After Gwyn's announcement everyone turned to him in amazement, and John Wilson was obviously very moved. On the morning of the concert I was rather nervous because I knew Gwyn had not performed for three years. Nick Bailey was presenting the concert and gave him a very big build-up. Gwyn appeared onstage with John Wilson and performed as well as I had ever heard him play. I was in tears, as were the artists and many of the audience because they knew the background. At the end of 'Rosie's Tune' Gwyn had a standing ovation and I was so pleased that our friend Chris Hancock had videoed this for the future.

After that there was no stopping Gwyn, because he decided to play in other concerts, in which he performed 'The Swan' by Saint-Saens and then 'Plaisir d'amour'. We had a classical Sail Away with all the artists involved, performing on deck as we left Vigo in Spain and, would you believe, Gwyn insisted on being part of it.

On the final day at sea we have an 'Encore' programme, when the artists perform music chosen by the passengers, from items they have heard during the cruise. Gwyn was Encored to perform 'Rosie's Tune' by John Wilson. Once again he performed brilliantly with the beautiful rich viola sound that he made. This was the last time he ever played the viola.

On the journey home from the cruise Gwyn said to me, "that was the best cruise ever, and there will never be another like it". I think he knew it would be his last.

A couple of months later Gwyn started to find eating more difficult and was losing weight again. On 21 April I tried to change Gwyn's valve, as this had to be changed regularly. This time the new valve would not go back into place. I tried a number of times and then told Gwyn I would have to plug, as I had been shown and we would have to go back to the hospital. When we arrived we saw Paul, one of our MacMillan nurses. He tried to fit the valve but to no avail. Gwyn had to be admitted to hospital that day for tests.

I was called to the hospital to hear the test results. Several nurses, both our MacMillan nurses, Paul and Mary, the oncologist and Doctor were all present around Gwyn's bed and he was told that nothing more could be done. I found this hard to take and left the room, with Mary following me, because I was sobbing my heart out. It was a very emotional time, and I had to give the girls this dreadful news. Mary said that Gwyn would need to go into a hospice but I wanted him at home with me. Both the girls arrived at the hospital and we talked about what should be done.

As the doctors had told me that I would not be able to cope at home, the girls thought this too. However, the next day the three of us got together and we decided Gwyn should come home. From that time onwards I stayed at the hospital and slept on a mattress, on the floor beside Gwyn's bed. I then started to learn how to do all the medical things I would need to do before Gwyn's return home.

I already knew how to clean the valve, which had to be done twice a day, but I needed to learn how to use a suction machine and also syringe his liquid food into his stomach, because of course he was unable to swallow. Once home there was also the oxygen to change each day. I did become quite proficient with all these things, so I then wanted Gwyn home as soon as possible.

In the event he came home on Wednesday 27 May. We had the conservatory made into a hospital ward, with the hospital bed and all the equipment. Gwyn loved to be able to look out at his garden, of which he was so proud. He never ever complained and always thanked everyone for what they did for him.

He never lost his sense of humour. On the day we returned home the Doctor arrived and informed Gwyn that he needed some penicillin for a little problem, and asked if he was allergic to anything. Gwyn just pointed to me! Dr Scrivens then said "You've not lost your sense of humour, Gwyn". We were very lucky to have such a good Doctor, two nurses twice a day from the Shakespeare Hospice, and two visits a day from the district nurses. They all loved Gwyn as everyone did. He could not speak but I became good at lip-reading. The Saturday before Gwyn died, my nephew Colin arrived to sit with him to watch the FA Cup Final (Lloyd, Julia's partner, had somehow raised up the television so Gwyn could see it easily), and Colin also managed to get him into a wheelchair to take him around his beloved garden.

We also had a visit from all the grandchildren a few days before he died, and he mimed to me "Wasn't it lovely to see all those lovely smiley faces". Little Charlie had picked some aubretia from the garden wall to give to Gwyn because he said he hadn't any other flowers to give him.

The Hospice nurses told me to expect the worst at any time, but he was holding on to life because he didn't want to go. Gwyn lost consciousness three days before he died and the girls were coming every day to see their father. Both were Daddy's girls and they loved him very much.

On the day Gwyn passed away, which was June 11th 2015, the girls were with him as usual in the morning. In the afternoon I played CDs as I had done since he lost consciousness. Rachel called me and said "where are you, Mum?" I replied "I am upstairs doing a few emails". She said that she thought I should go downstairs because she didn't think he had much longer.

I went downstairs and sat holding his hand. I looked at him and saw how thin he was, and thought it was cruel to wish him to go on any longer, so I held both his hands, after telling him several times how much I loved him and how much the girls loved him, I said "darling why don't you just slip away, we shall be fine, don't worry about us". With that he gave a couple of gasps and was gone and I know he heard me. I think he just was waiting for permission to go.

*   *   *

The funeral was a great celebration of Gwyn's life and it was a beautiful sunny day. As he was such a happy, smiley man I wanted everyone to wear bright colours for the funeral, and as he was a Manchester United fan Rachel's children wanted a ball of flowers and ribbon in Manchester United colours. The girls knew he loved purple and yellow flowers so they gave a cushion of purple and yellow flowers. Dan wanted a viola in flowers from Lucy and himself. I thought this would be difficult but we managed to get a beautiful viola made in flowers. I had a heart of red roses made, which I know he would have loved.

We had many friends involved in this celebration. John Wilson played the organ and wrote a piece for Gwyn entering the church. The coffin was carried by Dan, Henry and Harvey, at their request, with one of the pall bearers. Arwel Huw Morgan read a Dylan Thomas poem and sang 'Myfanwy' to remind us of Gwyn's Welsh roots. John Brearley played 'Rosie's Tune', Jean Kelly, harp and Alexei Sarkisov, cello, played 'The Swan', Maria Jagusz sang 'Ave Maria' and at the end of the service Yvonne sang 'You'll Never Walk Alone' because she had recently been singing it in the Opera North production of 'Carousel', and told me she was singing for Gwyn every night.

Nick Bailey gave a wonderful eulogy and both Henry and Harvey read messages from all the grandchildren. Even I managed to pay my own tribute to Gwyn. It was a long and perfect celebration of Gwyn's life with the church so full that many of the mourners were in the churchyard listening to it being recorded outside. Gwyn, being the humble man he was would have been so surprised that all this was for him.

Gwyn Williams Bursary

Gwyn would have hated us to end on a sad note so now it is the time to talk about the Gwyn Williams Bursary, which is his legacy. It is for young string players, but primarily for viola players at the Royal Birmingham Conservatoire.

With the help of many friends we launched the Gwyn Williams Bursary on Sunday 28 May 2017. This was held in the beautiful Town Hall in Birmingham, where Gwyn had started his career in Birmingham with the CBSO. Philip Head, a friend and colleague of Gwyn helped me to present a brilliant concert. Phil had been a first violin with the CBSO for many years but now fixes superb orchestras for events in the Midlands, including the orchestra every year for Longborough Festival Opera.

The whole event was hosted by Nick Bailey, the first voice of Classic FM Radio. Without hesitation he had agreed to introduce the evening as both he and his wife Frances had given us both tremendous support throughout the traumatic three and half years of Gwyn's illness. There could not have been a better presenter for this concert because Nick made it very personal and the feeling in the Hall was one of loving affection for Gwyn.

Yvonne Howard suggested that we include Vaughan Williams' 'Serenade to Music', and said she would organise the sixteen singers involved. These included professional opera singers who had been friends over the years and instrumentalists who had performed in the CBSO with Gwyn under Sir Simon Rattle; many had also performed with Gwyn on various occasions. Michael Seal agreed to conduct as he had been a colleague when he played violin in the CBSO. This was quite a coup as Mike is now in great demand as a conductor but he kept the date free and gave his services for this occasion.

The evening opened with Henry Fairs playing the Widor 'Toccata'. This was to be like a fanfare opening, but also showed off the magnificent organ situated in the Town Hall. The next work was Max Bruch's 'Romance for Viola and

Orchestra' with the strings of the Royal Birmingham Conservatoire conducted by Julian Lloyd Webber, with Yue Yu, a very talented young viola player who was studying at the RBC.

The concert was not without its crises, and in the morning Phil, three of my grandchildren and I were preparing for the afternoon rehearsal, due to start at 2pm. The timpani for 'Serenade to Music' were due to arrive at 10.30am so that the rest of the orchestral seating could be arranged once the timps were in place. Our great friend Tim from Maraca2 had hired the timps from Birmingham Conservatoire, because Tim and Jason, who made up Maraca2, were abroad at the time, and the hiring of the timps was their contribution towards the concert.

By 11am the timps had still not arrived so I went over to the Conservatoire to see what was happening. No one seemed to know about this so, after leaving notes, text messages and telephone calls for the lad who was organising this, I returned to the Town Hall. By this time it was after 12 noon, so Phil and I started to work on alternative arrangements as the timps were crucial for the Vaughan Williams work. Phil telephoned a percussion player and I started to look into other possibilities. As we were working out various options the timps arrived! The very apologetic young lad had forgotten about the timps but he eventually picked up my messages and got cracking. We quickly got the percussion in place and set the stage just in time for the rehearsal.

This was not the only problem. I had a message from the ConTempo String Quartet saying their flight from Dublin to Birmingham that morning had been delayed. This caused a minor panic but they arrived just in time for the 2pm rehearsal.

The Romanian Quartet ConTempo is quartet-in-residence for RTE Radio and Television and also quartet-in-residence in Galway. These four brilliant players had performed string quintets with Gwyn on the music cruises and they were great friends. They had offered their services to play in the orchestra throughout the evening and to play the Quartet part in Elgar's 'Introduction & Allegro'. In addition Andrea Bancui would play solo viola in the Howells 'Elegy' for Viola, String Quartet and Orchestra; the orchestra being the RBC strings, conducted by Mike Seal. The Quartet for this was ConTempo with Louise Lansdown, Head of Strings at the RBC playing the viola part. Louise was also interviewed by Nick to explain how the money for the Bursary would be used.

The orchestra for the 'Introduction and Allegro' was made up of Gwyn's CBSO and BSO colleagues plus solo instrumentalist friends who had all given their services for this concert. It was conducted by Mike Seal and it was hard to believe that there had only been one short afternoon rehearsal, as everyone was playing their hearts out for Gwyn. The sound was electric, ending the first half of the evening.

The second half began with Vaughan Williams' 'Serenade to Music'. For this we had a much larger orchestra again, made up of many friends and colleagues of Gwyn. Bogdon Sofei, first violin of the ConTempo Quartet played the solo violin part superbly. Again this was a brilliant performance and I think Mike Seal could not believe his luck in having sixteen of some of the best singers in the country performing the work, again on a very short afternoon rehearsal.

The rest of the programme consisted of solos that Gwyn had performed, including Chris Yates, viola section leader of the CBSO, playing 'Rosie's Tune' with Jean Kelly on the harp. This was the piece written by John Wilson and the last piece Gwyn ever played, and was followed by Alexei Sarkisov on cello performing 'The Swan' with Jean on harp. Jean had played this many times with Gwyn on music cruises.

To lighten the programme ConTempo played Romanian folk music in full Romanian Folk costume; Gwyn had loved The ConTempo rendition of this folk music. To bring the evening to a close Yvonne Howard sang 'Rule Britannia' with full orchestra, and the audience waving their Union Jack flags provided by P&O Cruises. Gwyn would have loved this grand finale, in which he had played so many times on the ship but also with CBSO on Proms Evenings.

At this stage the Gwyn Williams Bursary had not been set up, but the income from the concert enabled us to give £1,000 to MacMillan Nurses, £1,000 to the Shakespeare Hospice, and £1,000 third prize for the International Viola Competition held in Birmingham the following November. It also funded a talented young South African viola player to come from Soweto to attend all the sessions of the viola competition and perform in a concert in the Royal Birmingham Conservatoire. In addition there was still enough to pay for two viola students to attend music courses, which would not have been possible without the Bursary.

On the P&O Music cruises we sold Music Festival at Sea T-shirts with profits going to the Bursary and this has made more than £500 towards the fund.

After the success of the first event we needed to move forward, so in May 2019 another concert was given, this time in the Bradshaw Hall of the newly built Royal Birmingham Conservatoire. A musical weekend in the Crowne Plaza Hotel in Stratford upon Avon was organised for the Friends of Music Festivals at Sea. This was hosted by Nick and Frances Bailey, John Wilson, Peter O'Connor, Yvonne Howard and myself. It included a first night dinner, a CBSO concert the following night, and on the final evening the Gwyn Williams Bursary Concert.

The Bursary Concert in the Bradshaw Hall was another special event with mainly friends performing, but also students from the RBC. Our great friend Nick Bailey once again introduced the concert in his own inimitable style. The concert started with Christopher Yates, Gwyn's partner on the front desk of violas in the CBSO for many years, brilliantly performing Schubert's 'Arpeggione' Sonata with John Wilson at the piano. Yvonne Howard joined Chris and John in two very moving Brahms songs for mezzo, viola and piano. Bringing the first half to a conclusion, two students Yu-Che Chen, viola and Yang Bai, piano, gave a spectacular arrangement of the 'Dance of the Knights' from Prokofiev's 'Romeo and Juliet'.

The Behn Quartet gave an outstanding performance of the Smetana 'From my Life' String Quartet, which Gwyn loved playing, as it had so many brilliant viola solos. This was followed by Yvonne giving an affecting performance of Bellini's 'Casta Diva' accompanied by the Behn Quartet and Peter O'Connor on flute. John Wilson and Peter O'Connor ended the evening by performing 'The Carnival of Venice'. Pete wore a Carnival hat and turned the piece into a comedy act, which Gwyn would have loved.

This concert raised over £4,000 and has once again helped four Conservatoire viola students to attend music courses to develop their musicianship further.

Gwyn's aims were to encourage and nurture the careers of young musicians, and this Bursary for primarily young viola students helps to achieve this goal.

Sir Simon Rattle sums up this devoted and remarkable husband, father, grandfather and musician in his words below:

"Gwyn was a musician's musician. Of course he was a wonderful player, that goes without saying, but he was also permanently in a good mood which is much rarer! He was exactly the kind of colleague that all of us would wish for, enthusiastic, skilled and positive, and he remains embedded in all of our hearts.

Dear Gwyn, for all this and much more, our profound gratitude."

Simon Rattle

Simon Rattle. Photo credit: Oliver Helbig.

Appendix

MESSAGES

"Back in the 1990s I was recruited by Richard Baker's manager, Stephannie Williams … a lovely lady with organisational flair and savvy musical taste … to take over some of Richard's further-flung cruises on P&O ocean liners. Stephannie called her enjoyable operation the P&O Music Festival at Sea, and she organised three or four of them a year. It was far from being a conventional holiday, but we certainly saw the world, and I have always been grateful to Stephannie for introducing me to her scrupulously-planned ocean festivals."

Sir Humphrey Burton

* * *

"During my many earlier concerts with the CBSO, I well remember Gwyn Williams and the lovely chats we used to have, especially during and after rehearsals. He was seated immediately to my left when I was soloist and was always so cheerful … a lovely man! We had many amusing and entertaining conversations, and it was through him that I came to know his charming and attractive wife … Stephannie (Steve). Little did I realise what a skilled and successful organiser of concerts, tours and cruises she was.

Steve invited me to join her Music Team on no fewer than four highly enjoyable cruises. Each one was seamlessly and immaculately organised, thanks to her. She was always present, if and when required and continually showed great kindness and support to everyone. I heartily congratulate Steve and wish her all possible strength and continued success in the future. She remains an amazing example for others to try to emulate."

John Lill CBE

"Several years ago, when I was asked by a Sunday paper to write a travelogue on my first time aboard a cruise ship, I chose a P&O Classical Music cruise around the Baltic, and on boarding Aurora in Southampton, my wife and I were quickly adopted by the troupe of musicians and their leader, Stephannie Williams.

Steve's experience as performer, agent and producer of classical music is second-to-none and she has an instinct for bringing people together who will get on and work in quite a pressurised situation, producing a dozen different concerts from scratch over a three-week period, often through rough sea swells, with the ship's engines vibrating and groaning under the stage.

All are 'troupers', with Steve the biggest trouper of all. Her enthusiasm and high standards never droop, and the passengers appreciate every moment of the West End standard shows which they get to attend free of charge. My role is to greet the audience, relax and include them, and to introduce each piece. Because of the talents of the performers Steve assembles, I have the easiest job of all."

Kevin Whately

*   *   *

"I enjoyed so much working with Stephannie on the 'Sounds of Sweden' and 'Discover Denmark' Festivals she presented in Birmingham, collaborating with myself and Lyndon Jenkins. Her enthusiasm, vision and power of personality brought so many ideas into reality, and Birmingham was enhanced by the expertise and artistic quality of the many Nordic performers she brought to the city.

On a more personal level, we had such fun working together planning and going on the press trips prior to these festivals, whether to the home countries, or in bringing the press to Birmingham for the launches.

Steve was a wonderful colleague, and has been a vibrant contributor to the musical life of the West Midlands for many years. She made so many friends for Birmingham, and is remembered with much affection by at least equally as many from those abroad."

Andrew Jowett OBE
Former Director Symphony Hall and Town Hall, Birmingham

*   *   *

"I first met 'Steve' in 2004 over lunch at a Turkish restaurant next to the BBC where we discussed my forthcoming hosting of a Musical Festival at Sea. My first impression was of a very charming and attractive lady who belies her age, but as she also ran a concert agency I suspected she could be quite tough when need be. Once on the ship though I realised I couldn't have been in better hands as she guided me through that first cruise and helped to steady my nerves. I also met her husband Gwyn for the first time, who was equally charming. To date I've hosted twenty Music Festivals and in the process Steve and her late husband became valued friends. This is not to say I've never been told off but it was always done in such a gracious way that I almost looked forward to my dressing downs in her cabin!"

Nick Bailey

INDEX